GUN VIOLENCE

Fighting for Our Lives and Our Rights

Matt Doeden

TWENTY-FIRST CENTURY BOOKS / MINNEAPOLIS

Twenty-First Century Books
An imprint of Lerner Publishing Group, Inc.
241 First Avenue North
Minneapolis, MN 55401 USA

For reading levels and more information, look up this title at www.lernerbooks.com.

Main body text set in ITC Franklin Gothic Std.
Typeface provided by International Typeface Corporation.

Library of Congress Cataloging-in-Publication Data

Names: Doeden, Matt, author.
Title: Gun violence : fighting for our lives and our rights / Matt Doeden.
Description: Minneapolis : Twenty-First Century Books, [2020] | Includes
    bibliographical references and index. |
Identifiers: LCCN 2018054712 (print) | LCCN 2018060128 (ebook) |
    ISBN 9781541562677 (eb pdf) | ISBN 9781541555549 (lb : alk. paper)
Subjects: LCSH: Gun control—United States. | Firearms ownership—United
    States. | Firearms—Law and legislation—United States.
Classification: LCC HV7436 (ebook) | LCC HV7436 .D643 2020 (print) | DDC
    363.330973—dc23

LC record available at https://lccn.loc.gov/2018054712

Manufactured in the United States of America
1-46009-42926-3/12/2019

CONTENTS

Chapter 1
MARCH FOR OUR LIVES // 4

Chapter 2
THE HISTORY OF US GUN RIGHTS // 10

Chapter 3
A QUESTION OF SAFETY // 34

Chapter 4
WHO SHOULD OWN GUNS? // 52

Chapter 5
ARE ALL FIREARMS CREATED EQUAL? // 66

Chapter 6
MEASURES OF CONTROL // 78

Timeline // 96

Glossary // 99

Source Notes // 100

Selected Bibliography // 104

Further Information // 104

Index // 108

Chapter I

MARCH FOR OUR LIVES

Marchers filled the streets of Washington, DC, on March 24, 2018. Tens of thousands of people—mostly teenagers—carried signs and chanted as they walked along Pennsylvania Avenue. The mass of protesters stretched along the avenue from the US Capitol to the White House and beyond. They were part of one of the largest protests in the United States since the Vietnam War (1957–1975). A little more than a month before the march, on February 14, a lone shooter had entered Marjory Stoneman Douglas High School in Parkland, Florida. In just over six minutes, the nineteen-year-old shooter (a former student at the school) killed seventeen people and wounded many more. He did so with an assault rifle that he had purchased legally under US and Florida gun laws. The March for Our Lives was a response to gun violence, especially to this and other school shootings. The students, as well as many adult allies, were there to send a message to politicians.

The protest march was mirrored in cities around the nation and the globe. In New York, young people dressed in orange—the color hunters wear for visibility—and marched through

Emma González (*center*) and others organized the March for Our Lives event in Washington, DC, in March 2018.

Central Park. Columbine, Colorado, was the site of another high-profile protest. The first major school shooting in the United States occurred in Columbine. Students gathered on a soccer field to release balloons in memory of shooting victims. In Paris, France, marchers chanted, "Hey hey, ho ho, gun violence has got to go!"

School shootings and other mass shootings have become an epidemic in the United States. According to the advocacy group Everytown for Gun Safety, the violence at Marjory Stoneman Douglas was the fifty-eighth school shooting in the United States since 2014. For the Parkland students, enough was enough. Fresh from the pain of losing friends, they took a high-profile stand against gun violence. People around the world rallied to their cause. The March for Our Lives event was the culmination of the students' earliest efforts to organize. They directed their anger and message at US lawmakers. The message also was aimed at powerful organizations such as the National Rifle Association (NRA) that oppose most gun-control measures.

"If you listen real close, you can hear the people in power shaking," said David Hogg, one of the students who had survived the Parkland shooting. He spoke to the crowd gathered outside the Capitol Building in Washington, DC. "We're going to take this to every election, to every state and every city. We're going to make sure the best people get in our elections to run, not as politicians but as Americans."

Nine-year-old Yolanda Renee King, the granddaughter of civil rights leader Martin Luther King Jr., spoke at the Capitol too. "I have a dream that enough is enough," she said, mirroring the famous words of her grandfather more than half a century earlier. "That this should be a gun-free world. Period."

The marchers enjoyed a groundswell of support and media coverage. Yet not all Americans agree with their message. Opponents believe strongly that the right to bear arms is an important and cherished guarantee of the US Constitution's Bill of Rights as spelled out in the Second Amendment. These Americans feel that government should not limit gun rights at all, or if it does, only minimally. A handful of marchers turned out to oppose the March for Our Lives protests to spread their own message. In Salt Lake City, Utah, for example, marchers waved flags and carried pistols. In Utah the law allows people to carry firearms openly and concealed, as long as they have a permit and meet other requirements to do so. One marcher carried a sign that read, "What can we do to stop mass shootings? SHOOT BACK."

The Parkland incident rekindled a debate that has raged for decades in the United States. Should anyone be able to own

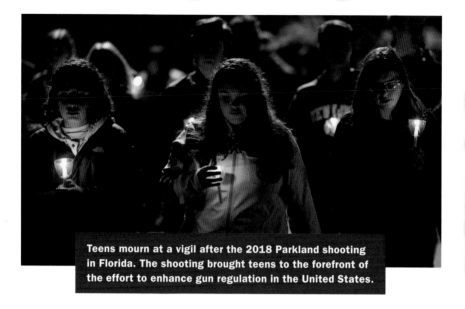

Teens mourn at a vigil after the 2018 Parkland shooting in Florida. The shooting brought teens to the forefront of the effort to enhance gun regulation in the United States.

powerful firearms, or should government limit gun rights? Are guns a danger to society, or do they protect us from criminals and help guarantee freedom for all?

THE RIGHT TO KEEP AND BEAR ARMS

Gun control is a complex and hotly debated issue in the United States. The Second Amendment is part of the US Constitution, a document that defines the basic principles and laws of the United States. This amendment guarantees the American people the right to keep and bear arms. But what does this really mean? What did the founders intend when they wrote this guarantee more than two hundred years ago? And how does it apply to twenty-first-century society and high-tech weaponry that the nation's founders could never have envisioned?

A gun in the wrong hands can be deadly. According to the US Department of Health and Human Services, about thirty thousand people die in the United States each year from gunshot wounds. This figure includes murders, suicides, and accidents. Proponents, or supporters, of gun control say that the issue is simple: More guns in society cause more gun-related deaths. They say that children, criminals, and people with serious mental illnesses shouldn't have easy access to guns. They believe that private citizens have no reason or need to own assault rifles and other high-powered weapons of war.

Gun-rights supporters often counter this argument by saying that guns don't kill people—people kill people. They mean that

THE SECOND AMENDMENT

Gun rights in the United States ultimately boil down to interpretations of the Second Amendment to the US Constitution—one of ten basic liberties outlined in the Bill of Rights. The Second Amendment reads, "A well regulated Militia, being necessary to the security of a free State, the right of the people to keep and bear Arms, shall not be infringed."

The wording of the Second Amendment is brief and not entirely clear. Many historians note that the founders' main intent in writing this amendment was to allow militias (small, local, and loosely organized military groups) to exist. The young United States did not have a standing army. Militias provided the nation's only organized defense. So protecting militias and the nation's right to call them to arms was important. Some scholars suggest that the Second Amendment refers to the public's collective right to own arms, not to individual gun rights.

Other historians focus on the phrase "the right of the people to keep and bear Arms." They believe this phrase suggests that the Second Amendment was intended to guarantee all citizens the right to own whatever guns they want. The preamble (introduction) about militias is irrelevant, they say. The guarantee is all that matters.

The vague nature of the Second Amendment may not have been particularly important when it was written. But gun technology has changed and weapons of increasingly destructive power are mass-produced. So an understanding of the amendment and its guarantees has become the center of the gun-control debate. Just what did the founders intend with the Second Amendment? Lawmakers have struggled to answer this question for more than two centuries.

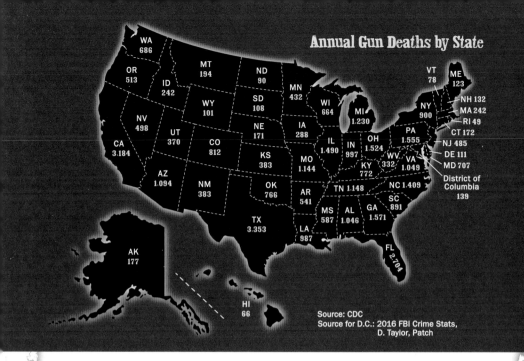

WA 686
OR 513
MT 194
ND 90
ID 242
MN 432
VT 78
ME 123
WY 101
SD 108
WI 664
NY 900
NH 132
NV 498
UT 370
NE 171
IA 288
MI 1.230
PA 1.555
MA 242
RI 49
CA 3.184
CO 812
IL 1.490
IN 997
OH 1.524
CT 172
NJ 485
AZ 1.094
KS 383
MO 1.144
WV 332
KY 772
VA 1.049
DE 111
MD 707
NM 383
OK 766
AR 541
TN 1.148
NC 1.409
District of Columbia 139
TX 3.353
MS 587
AL 1.046
GA 1.571
SC 891
LA 987
FL 2.704
AK 177
HI 66

Source: CDC
Source for D.C.: 2016 FBI Crime Stats, D. Taylor, Patch

guns are tools. The shooters—not their guns—are to blame for gun-related deaths. They also point out that millions of gun owners are law-abiding citizens. These gun owners use guns only for hunting, target shooting, and self-defense. They know how to use guns properly, and they take the necessary safety precautions for using and storing guns. Those who oppose gun restrictions view the right to bear arms as an important part of what makes Americans free.

How can society preserve the right of responsible citizens to own weapons while keeping guns away from dangerous people? That's the crux of the gun-control debate, and there are no easy answers.

"The Second Amendment gives you the right to bear arms. But really, that's the beginning point of the conversation. As is true with most of the Bill of Rights, the intent is not totally clear, and in fact, the language in the Second Amendment is particularly confusing."
—Jesse Choper, retired law professor, University of California, Berkeley, 2017

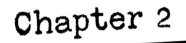

Chapter 2

THE HISTORY OF US GUN RIGHTS

The issue of controlling access to weapons isn't new—nor is it unique to the United States. People have argued over it for centuries. For example, in the twelfth century CE, a debate raged in Europe over crossbows. These weapons are mechanized bows that fire short, heavy, pointed projectiles called bolts. The weapon is much deadlier than an ordinary bow that shoots arrows. In 1139 nearly one thousand high-ranking Roman Catholic clerics met in Rome for the Second Lateran Council. There, the religious leaders agreed to thirty canons, or rules and regulations, to guide the church and its followers. In the twenty-ninth canon, the council banned the crossbow. In one translation of the canons, the clerics described it as "a weapon hateful to God" and "too lethal for Christians to use against one another." Despite this condemnation, European armies— Christian and otherwise—continued to use the crossbow.

This illustration depicts medieval archers with crossbows and different types of arrows.

People began to use modern firearms such as cannons and guns in the fourteenth century. Early firearms used gunpowder, an explosive chemical mixture, to launch small projectiles from tubelike enclosures. Such firearms originated in China and then spread to the Middle East and Europe. At first, the gun was mainly a curiosity and not particularly useful in battle. Early guns were unreliable and inaccurate. Their range was short, and loading them was time-consuming. Gunpowder also required careful handling. A soldier had to pack loose gunpowder into the barrel of the gun. If gunpowder separated into its individual chemicals or was distributed unevenly inside the gun, the gunpowder would not explode, and the weapon was useless. Proven weapons such as blades and bows were much more reliable and efficient.

EVOLVING GUNS, EVOLVING ATTITUDES

For centuries guns remained a fringe technology. They weren't reliable enough to use on the battlefield. But inventors continued to experiment with and improve on gun design. They also developed new methods of preparing gunpowder, such as baking it into pellets. A soldier could quickly load pellets into his gun. Pellets were also much more reliable than loose gunpowder, with low rates of malfunction.

By the sixteenth century, pistols, or handguns, and long guns such as the harquebus were common. Yet guns were still largely ineffective. Seasoned warriors scoffed at guns, seeing them as crude and clumsy. Many people of the day viewed gun users as cowards. A true warrior relied on his blade—a weapon that required both skill and courage. Using a gun required little skill and even less courage, critics said.

Although guns and their users earned little respect for centuries, improving technology eventually made them impossible to ignore. From the sixteenth through the eighteenth centuries, gun design advanced rapidly. Long-barreled guns called muskets brought greater range and accuracy. Fitted with blades called bayonets, muskets were useful for both long-range and close combat. Soon armies could not survive without guns.

While guns earned grudging acceptance as a military necessity, they remained largely unacceptable in civilian (nonmilitary) society. In Europe wealthy upper-class members of society saw guns as a threat to their power. If common people had guns, they could easily revolt against their rulers. Therefore, many European nations strictly controlled guns. In 1594, for example, Queen Elizabeth I of England banned a type of gun called the wheel-lock pistol because it was easy to hide and to carry loaded.

But many of these gun restrictions were unnecessary, because guns were very expensive and difficult to use. Fear of poor people arising en masse, or all together, with guns in hand was unrealistic. Few people could afford guns, and fewer still knew how to load and fire them. The restrictions didn't do much. But they did establish a social and legal precedent, or model, of people in power keeping guns away from the common people.

GUNS IN NORTH AMERICA

As gun technology evolved, Europeans were opening new frontiers to expand their economies and global power. European explorers, soldiers, and settlers began flocking to the Americas in the sixteenth century. England, France, Spain, Portugal, and other European nations sent shiploads of white settlers across the Atlantic Ocean. Each nation was determined to take land and set up colonies in the Americas. Some of the colonists came armed with guns. They used them to drive indigenous (Native American) peoples off the land they wanted.

As colonists set up territories and began to create successful industries, wealth in the Americas grew. The cost of guns fell, and a culture of guns developed that had never existed in Europe. To many colonists, guns were a necessity in a land they saw as wild and dangerous. Europeans and American Indians frequently clashed violently over control of land. Colonists wanted guns to defend themselves and their claim to land. Gun ownership became a way of life.

As Europeans expanded their settlements in the Americas, firearms played a key role in the conquest of indigenous peoples. Gun-wielding Europeans had an advantage over American Indians bearing only bows, clubs, spears, and knives. Guns were fast and efficient, and they were effective at long range. American Indians saw the advantage and wanted guns of their own. So firearms became important trading goods between colonists and American Indians.

By the eighteenth century, thirteen British colonies dominated the eastern seaboard along the Atlantic coast of North America. Citizens of these colonies lived under the rule of the British king, but their lives were quite different from those of their fellow subjects in Great Britain. Gun ownership was one of many differences. In Europe guns remained restricted to society's elite. Laws still prevented common people from owning or using firearms. Yet in the early years of British colonial rule, British rulers encouraged gun ownership among North American colonists. They did this because the colonists weren't a direct threat to their rulers across the ocean and so that armed colonists could defend themselves. They didn't require British troops to come to the colonies to keep them safe. The British Empire saved huge amounts of money by allowing North American colonists to defend themselves.

While gun ownership was widespread in North America, it wasn't unregulated. For example, in some colonies, able-bodied men who refused to serve in militias were not allowed to own weapons. Black slaves and other minorities could not carry firearms in any colony. A 1723 Virginia law read, "No negro [black person], mulatto [mixed-race person], or Indian [indigenous person] whatsoever . . . shall hereafter presume to keep, or carry any gun, powder, shot, or any club, or other weapon whatsoever, offensive or defensive." Such laws helped keep power in the hands of white people.

THE AMERICAN REVOLUTION

Throughout the eighteenth century, the thirteen colonies grew more self-sufficient. They also became resentful of British interference in their lives. Great Britain was fighting the French and Indian War (1754–1763) against the French and several American Indian nations over territory along the western frontier of the colonies. Great Britain looked for ways to pay for its military expenses. The solution: higher taxes on the American colonists.

The tax increase did not go over well in the colonies. Anti-British sentiment grew into widespread protests. Colonists complained that Great Britain was taxing them without giving them any say in colonial lawmaking. By contrast, their fellow citizens in Great Britain had some say in British government.

In the 1770s, tensions reached a breaking point, and fighting erupted in Massachusetts in 1775 between colonists and British soldiers. The next year, the thirteen colonies banded together and declared independence from Great Britain. They formed a new nation, the United States of America, and rejected British rule. Great Britain would not let its colonies go without a fight. And so the American Revolution (1775–1783) began.

The colonies' gun culture played a major role in the war. The fledgling United States had no stockpiles of weapons for its new military force, the Continental Army. Many Continental soldiers supplied their own weapons. Many new militias formed across the colonies. They consisted of local men, many of whom owned guns. These militias contributed to the fight against the British. Therefore, many early Americans celebrated gun ownership not only as a US citizen's right but also as a citizen's obligation. Owning a gun was an act of patriotism. Guns became a symbol of the fierce independence of the young United States.

Supplying US troops with guns was a constant struggle for General George Washington, leader of the Continental Army, and for his officers. While many Americans owned guns, most of the weapons were in poor condition and were not suitable for military use. This was especially true in frontier areas, which had fewer white settlements and were farther from ports and markets. Because of the shortage of suitable guns, US troops often carried other weapons instead, such as bows, spears, and hatchets. Later in the war, guns imported from Europe helped turn the tide in the Continental Army's favor.

Washington didn't have enough guns to supply his whole army until the early 1780s. Victory came as soon as he got the needed weapons from Europe. US troops forced a British surrender in 1781, ending the war in North America. A formal peace treaty followed in 1783. A new nation was born. It was time to lay out the law of the land, and the right to own guns would be a big part of it.

GUN LAWS IN THE NEW NATION

The United States adopted its Constitution in 1787, but many lawmakers and citizens were dissatisfied with the document. It lacked language to guarantee certain personal freedoms.

So lawmakers added ten amendments, or changes, to the Constitution in 1791. These amendments, called the Bill of Rights, describe the specific rights of US citizens. The Bill of Rights prevents the government from denying important individual freedoms.

The new US government and state governments had many decisions to make about the laws of the new nation. The US Constitution was adopted in 1787, and by 1790, the thirteen states had ratified it. A year later, the Second Amendment, protecting gun rights, became part of the Bill of Rights. Yet leaders continued to struggle with the issue of gun policy. After the war, the United States was full of guns and people who knew how to use them. Some leaders favored laws like those in Europe, which limited gun rights. Others pointed to the central role that private citizens—and their guns—had played in the war. These leaders argued that all Americans should have the right to bear arms with no restrictions.

Senator Rufus King of New York fell into the camp that supported gun control. In 1790 he argued before the US Senate "that it was dangerous to put arms into the hands of the frontier people for their defense [for fear] they should use them against the United States." This opinion had some justification. The United States had already faced rebellions, including Shays' Rebellion in 1786, when poor farmers in western Massachusetts took up arms against local courts and tax collectors.

Others took the opposite view. Among them was Virginia politician Thomas Jefferson, who wrote, "What country can preserve its liberties if their rulers are not warned from time to time that their people preserve the spirit of resistance? Let them take arms. . . . The tree of liberty must be refreshed from time to time with the blood of patriots and tyrants." Jefferson was saying that an armed citizenry was an effective way to guard against a cruel and oppressive government.

The details and nature of gun rights eventually found their way into federal and state laws. Many of these laws focused more on a government's right to call and arm militias than on personal gun rights. But they set an important legal precedent about gun control.

EVOLVING GUN LAW

For a century after the Bill of Rights was ratified, Americans largely ignored the Second Amendment. Gun technology changed little during that time, and the nation didn't seek further gun legislation. Yet gun violence was common. For example, gunfights in the western territories were an everyday affair. Duels often solved disputes in the South. In these strictly regulated contests, combatants fought, often to the death, with pistols or other weapons. In other cases, gun use was more chaotic. In 1873, for example, an election dispute erupted in Louisiana. A white mob, angry at the results of a local election, attacked a group of African Americans protecting the courthouse in the town of Colfax. The mob badly outgunned the armed black citizens. After a brief fight, they threw down their arms and surrendered. The white mob murdered almost all the African Americans.

The absolute right of US citizens to own guns went unchallenged for the next half century. Meanwhile, gun technology and manufacture progressed at a rapid rate as mechanization took hold in the United States. By the 1920s, guns were no longer the inaccurate, slow-loading beasts of centuries past. Long-barreled and breech-loading (front end) rifles shot spinning bullets with stunning accuracy. Guns became smaller so that people could carry and fire pocket-sized handguns easily. Automatic weapons technology allowed users to fire multiple rounds of ammunition with a single pull of the trigger. Meanwhile, organized crime was on the rise. As criminals armed themselves with increasingly powerful weapons, many legislators believed it was time for gun laws to catch up with gun technology.

The US Congress passed its first law restricting guns in 1927. The Mailing of Firearms Act outlawed the shipping of concealable handguns by US mail. Mail-order sales had taken off in the early twentieth century, and the law's main purpose was to slow mail-order gun sales to members of organized crime groups. Most politicians supported this small step, though criminals easily skirted it. But it marked the beginning of a new era of gun-control efforts. The age of unchallenged gun rights in the United States was over.

FIREARMS LEGISLATION

Public fear about organized crime continued into the 1930s. Crime groups were growing ever bigger and bolder, using weapons of terrible power: sawed-off shotguns that could hide inside a coat, tommy guns (lightweight machine guns), and more. Criminals often outgunned the police, imperiling both the police and the public.

In 1934 the US Congress proposed new legislation to deal with the problem. The National Firearms Act taxed the sales of certain weapons, including handguns, short-barreled rifles and shotguns, automatic weapons, silencers, and explosive devices. It also required registration of all such weapons with federal authorities. Few Americans opposed the regulation of automatic weapons and bombs. But including handguns in the proposed law set off a firestorm of protest. The National Rifle Association (NRA), a gun-rights group founded in 1871, organized a letter-writing campaign objecting to the inclusion of those guns in the bill. It worked. Congress altered the law, leaving handguns out of it.

The National Firearms Act of 1934 proved ineffective at controlling gun violence. So Congress introduced the Federal Firearms Act of 1938 as a more comprehensive gun-control bill. The original draft called for gun owners to register their guns and to have gun licenses. Supporters argued that the bill did not infringe upon the Second Amendment. It preserved the right to bear arms—with the proper documentation. But the NRA saw things differently and protested loudly and effectively. Congress stripped down the bill. The version that passed into law accomplished several objectives. It banned the sale of firearms to convicted felons (people convicted of serious crimes) and fugitives (people on the run from the law). It outlawed the transport or shipping of firearms whose serial numbers had been removed or altered to make them difficult to track. And it barred unlicensed dealers from selling guns across state lines. This licensing issue was a token gesture, however, as the cost of licensing was a paltry one dollar.

A REVIVED DEBATE

In the 1930s, Americans struggled during the global economic collapse of the Great Depression (1929–1942). Banks closed, industries failed, and millions of Americans lost their jobs, their savings, and their homes. The United States joined World War II (1939–1945) in 1941. For the next four years, the nation dedicated itself to the war. The economy got a much-needed jump start as Americans went back to work at new factories for manufacturing everything the US military needed to fight the war. Organized crime declined, and the gun-control debate quieted for the next twenty years.

THE NATIONAL RIFLE ASSOCIATION

During the Civil War, two Union officers, William Church and George Wingate, were shocked by their troops' poor marksmanship. So, in 1871, the two men formed the National Rifle Association to promote rifle shooting and improve marksmanship among American gun owners.

The early NRA bore little resemblance to the political organization it would later become. It focused on building shooting ranges and promoting sport shooting. In the first decade of the twentieth century, the NRA began encouraging youth shooting programs and college rifle clubs. In 1916 the NRA took control of a firearms interest magazine, *Arms and the Man,* changing its name in 1923 to the *American Rifleman.* One purpose of the magazine was to inform NRA members of gun laws under consideration around the nation.

In 1934 the NRA formed a legislative affairs division to fight against perceived attacks on Second Amendment rights. This new wing of the NRA helped organize protests and letter-writing campaigns to pressure politicians into voting down laws restricting gun ownership. The NRA's political clout grew over the following decades. Through the late 1960s, the NRA supported some level of gun control. But passage of the Gun Control Act of 1968 created a rift among NRA leaders. Some supported modest gun control, and others opposed it in all forms.

By the mid-1970s, opposition to all gun control prevailed, cementing the NRA's hard-line stance. The NRA's lobbying power grew. By 2017 the NRA claimed to have a national membership of five million people. While that's less than one-fifth of American gun owners, the organization raises millions of dollars each year, often from small donations, and wields enormous political influence.

The debate reemerged in 1963. Senator Thomas Dodd of Connecticut was on a US Senate committee dealing with youth crime. He blamed easy access to cheap imported handguns for contributing to the problem. He proposed making these cheap handguns more difficult and expensive to get by heavily taxing imported handguns. But historians think that Dodd may have had an additional motive. Dodd's home state was a hub of gun manufacturing. His proposal would have helped US gun manufacturers, who were losing sales to foreign gun makers.

Shortly after Dodd made his proposal, a tragedy shook the nation. Lee Harvey Oswald assassinated President John F. Kennedy in Dallas, Texas, on November 22, 1963. Oswald had used an imported Italian rifle to kill the young and popular president. He had ordered the inexpensive rifle after seeing an advertisement in the NRA's magazine, the *American Rifleman.* Dodd responded to the assassination by widening the scope of his bill to include mail-order rifles and handguns. Congress defeated the bill, largely because many lawmakers thought it was too sweeping.

Five years later, Congress passed the Gun Control Act of 1968. This act was a response to a series of violent urban riots and political assassinations, including the murders of civil rights leader Martin Luther King Jr. and Senator Robert Kennedy of New York, President Kennedy's brother. Unlike the bills before it, this legislation had some teeth. It severely restricted gun and ammunition sales across state lines. It required gun dealers to keep detailed records of every sale. It banned the import of guns not used for sports such as hunting or target shooting. It established a federal regulatory agency, later called the Bureau of Alcohol, Tobacco, Firearms and Explosives. The Gun Control Act of 1968 was the first comprehensive gun legislation ever passed in the United States.

The act was controversial. Some felt that comprehensive gun legislation was long overdue and that this law was just a beginning. Others claimed it infringed on Second Amendment rights. The debate raged even within the NRA. One top NRA official reportedly favored the legislation. Others opposed it. The divide created a power struggle within the organization. Some members wanted to support reasonable gun control, while others opposed gun-control legislation of any kind. Eventually the group opposed to any legislation took control of the NRA. Opposition to almost all gun control has remained the NRA's position ever since.

POLITICAL TUG-OF-WAR

Over the following decades, gun control became more politicized. The NRA grew into a large and powerful political force. It used its size and wealth to lobby, or influence, politicians and other officials to support eased restrictions on gun sales. In elections the NRA usually supported conservative gun-rights candidates. NRA support forced a divide between conservatives (mostly Republicans) and liberals (mostly Democrats) on the issue.

In the early 1980s, controversy surrounded armor-piercing bullets. These bullets blast through armor such as bulletproof vests. Some people call such bullets "cop killers" because criminals used them to kill police officers. Congress introduced bills to ban the sales of such bullets, but the NRA fought the ban. It claimed the ban would limit hunters' ammunition choices. But even many of the NRA's longtime political allies questioned that claim. One senator reportedly asked when deer had started wearing body armor. The bullets were unnecessary for hunting and were used mainly to kill people, especially police officers. Congress reached a compromise in the Law Enforcement Officers Protection Act of 1985. The law forbade US manufacture of and import of armor-piercing ammunition except for government use.

In 1986 the NRA scored a major victory in its battle against gun control. That year, due mostly to NRA persistence, the US Congress passed the Firearm Owners' Protection Act. This law scaled back many of the 1968 restrictions on gun dealers. It lifted the ban on interstate sales. It more narrowly defined the term *gun dealer* so that dealer restrictions applied to fewer gun sellers. And it allowed licensed dealers to sell at gun shows. As a compromise, the law banned machine guns made after 1986.

Other laws were in the works too. For example, two US senators sponsored a bill called the Undetectable Firearms Act of 1988. If passed, this law would have banned all-plastic guns, which can evade metal detectors. The bill never came to a vote.

THE BRADY BILL

The next major gun-control debate started in 1987, when the Brady Handgun Violence Prevention Act was introduced in Congress. This proposal stemmed from the attempted assassination of President Ronald Reagan six years earlier. John Hinckley Jr. had opened fire on Reagan and others near a hotel in Washington, DC. Reagan took a bullet in his lung and recovered quickly. His press secretary, James Brady, wasn't so lucky. A bullet struck him in the head. The bullet was designed to shatter on impact. It sent metal fragments into Brady's brain. Brady survived the attack, but the wound left him with a permanent brain injury and partial paralysis.

Later, Brady and his wife led a new campaign for gun control. They formed an organization called the Brady Campaign to Prevent Gun Violence. In the 1980s, its members lobbied for a waiting period for gun purchases. They proposed that anyone buying a gun should have a seven-day waiting period before receiving the gun. They argued that a waiting period would prevent people from rushing out in anger or confusion to buy guns and commit crimes. It would also give police time to do background checks and prevent convicted felons and illegal immigrants from buying guns. The proposal wouldn't prevent anyone from buying a gun. It would just slow down the process.

James Brady (*seated far left*) and his family (*back row center right*) attended President Bill Clinton's signing of the Brady Act into law in 1993. The law mandates a waiting period between purchasing a gun and taking the weapon into a person's possession.

The NRA protested, claiming that a waiting period would not prevent violent criminals from obtaining guns. The NRA pointed out that criminals often buy guns from individuals, not from licensed gun dealers. The waiting period, they argued, would do little more than make it harder for law-abiding gun owners to purchase guns. After a long and heated debate, the Brady Act finally passed—with some alterations—in 1993. The seven-day waiting period shrank to five days. And the waiting-period requirement would expire in 1998. Meanwhile, the Federal Bureau of Investigation (FBI) would set up an instant background check system that would go into effect once the waiting period expired in 1998.

DISTRICT OF COLUMBIA v. HELLER

In 1994, just one year after the Brady Act passed into law, the gun-control debate reemerged over assault weapons. These powerful automatic or semiautomatic weapons are designed for military-style attacks. That year Congress passed the Violent Crime Control and Law Enforcement Act. Among other things, this law banned many of the world's most common assault weapons, listing them by name rather than by broader categories. The federal assault weapons ban expired in 2004, and Congress did not renew it. Since then proposals for new assault weapons bans have come and gone. None has passed.

The gun-control debate heated up again in 2007 and 2008. A few years earlier, residents of Washington, DC, had mounted a legal challenge against the city's gun-control law. This law banned most residents from owning handguns, automatic firearms, high-capacity semiautomatic weapons, and unregistered firearms. The law also required firearms in private homes to be unloaded, disassembled, or stored in a locked cabinet or safe. The case, called *District of Columbia v. Heller,* rose all the way to the US Supreme Court. The key question was whether the Second Amendment protects individual gun rights or the collective gun rights of all Americans.

In June 2008, the Supreme Court reached a decision. For the majority opinion, Justice Antonin Scalia wrote, "The Second Amendment protects an individual right to possess a firearm unconnected with service in a militia, and to use that arm for traditionally lawful purposes, such as self-defense within the home." Writing separate opinions for the dissent, Justices Stephen Breyer and John Paul Stevens said that the amendment does not protect an absolute right to gun ownership. The NRA and other gun-rights supporters hailed the ruling as a major victory.

MASS SHOOTINGS

In 2012 a twenty-year-old gunman entered Sandy Hook Elementary School in Newton, Connecticut. He killed twenty

THE COLUMBINE SHOOTINGS

On the morning of April 20, 1999, students and teachers filled the halls of Columbine High School in Columbine, Colorado. For most of them, the day started like any other. But later that morning, as gunshots rang through the school, the day became one that many Americans will never forget.

The shooters were two Columbine students, Eric Harris and Dylan Klebold, later described as social outcasts. They had been in trouble with the law before. They had made threats against classmates and committed other petty, or minor, crimes.

They were too young to purchase firearms legally, so an older friend bought a semiautomatic rifle and two shotguns for them at a gun show. Another contact later sold them a semiautomatic handgun. The boys also built a supply of homemade explosive devices at their homes.

In the late morning of April 20, Klebold and Harris killed one teacher and twelve students and injured another twenty-one students. Harris and Klebold ended their shooting spree by taking their own lives. The story made news worldwide. Questions swirled. What had caused these boys to go on a deadly rampage? And how had they acquired such powerful firearms?

The boys each had a history of criminal behavior. Both had undergone psychological treatment for emotional problems. Every warning sign was up. Gun-control activists quickly portrayed the tragedy as evidence that US gun laws were too lax. Gun-rights supporters pointed out that existing gun-control laws hadn't prevented Harris and Klebold from getting the guns they wanted. More laws would do no good.

An impromptu memorial arose at a park in Littleton, Colorado, shortly after a school shooting at nearby Columbine High School in April 1999.

The Columbine shootings marked the beginning of a dark new era in gun violence. Copycat killers began staging their own school shootings. Within a decade, school shootings had grown into an epidemic, with no end in sight.

children, between the ages of six and seven, and six adults before taking his own life. Four years later, in 2016, a twenty-nine-year-old security guard killed forty-nine people in a gay nightclub in Orlando, Florida. A year later, a sixty-four-year-old man opened fire from a hotel window onto a crowd at a music festival in Las Vegas, killing fifty-nine people (including himself) and injuring almost one thousand more. Then, in February 2018, a teen gunman killed seventeen people at Marjory Stoneman Douglas High School in Parkland, Florida. In October 2018, a forty-six-year-old man gunned down eleven people at a Jewish synagogue in Pittsburgh, Pennsylvania. These were just a few of what many Americans saw as an epidemic of mass shootings.

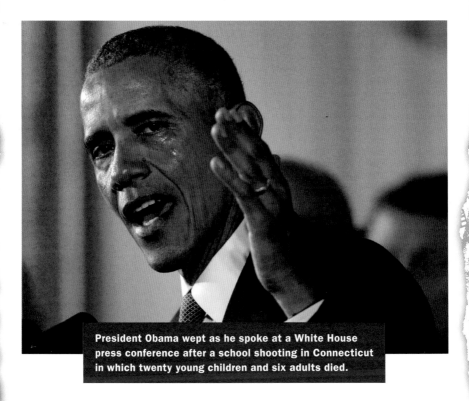

President Obama wept as he spoke at a White House press conference after a school shooting in Connecticut in which twenty young children and six adults died.

THE PULSE NIGHTCLUB SHOOTING

The idea of terrorists with guns gives pause to even the most passionate gun-rights supporters. That aspect of the gun-control debate took center stage on June 12, 2016. That evening a shooter who claimed allegiance to a radical Islamic organization walked into Pulse, a gay nightclub in Orlando, Florida, and opened fire. The attack left fifty people dead, including the shooter, and marked the biggest terrorist attack on US soil since the September 11, 2001, terror attacks in New York City and near Washington, DC.

In the days right after the shooting, many Americans believed that the shooter had carried out a hate crime targeting gay people. But later evidence suggests that the shooter wasn't aware of that, having asked a security guard why there weren't any women inside.

The shooter used a Sig MCX, a semiautomatic assault-style rifle that resembles the AR-15. He had purchased the weapon, along with other firearms, legally. Gun-control supporters quickly pointed out that the AR-15 had been used in previous mass shootings. They called for further restriction

Mourners gathered in Orlando after the deadly terrorist shooting at the Pulse nightclub in June 2016. Many Americans initially believed the shooting was a hate crime, but evidence suggests the killer was not aware that the club attracted a gay clientele.

on such assault rifles. Gun-rights supporters countered that banning this type of weapon would not stop mass shootings. They said that focusing on issues such as terrorism and mental health were more important than restricting gun rights.

"The United States of America is not the only country on Earth with violent or dangerous people. We are not inherently more prone to violence. But we are the only advanced country on Earth that sees this kind of mass violence erupt with this kind of frequency. It doesn't happen in other advanced countries. It's not even close. . . . And instead of thinking about how to solve the problem, this has become one of our most polarized, partisan debates—despite the fact that there's a general consensus in America about what needs to be done."
—President Barack Obama, 2016

Waves of protest and calls for changes to gun laws came from anguished parents, survivors, and allies after each shooting. Among the loudest of them came in 2018 after the Parkland shooting. For the first time in the history of the gun-control debate, teens took the lead in demanding change. As young people—led by survivors of the Parkland shooting—mobilized and demanded change, politicians on both sides of the debate scrambled to come up with solutions. The March for Our Lives protests in March 2018 highlighted the teen-led movement, with marches across the nation and the globe. Republican president Donald Trump was quick to advocate further gun laws, especially regarding universal background checks. "We want to pass something great, and to me the something great has to be where we prevent it from happening again," Trump said, referring to the Parkland shooting.

His call to action was short-lived, however. Shortly afterward, Trump addressed members at the NRA's annual convention in Dallas, Texas. He told them, "Your Second Amendment rights are under siege. But they will never, ever be

TRAYVON MARTIN

On February 26, 2012, seventeen-year-old Trayvon Martin was visiting relatives in the Twin Lakes gated community in Sanford, Florida. As Martin walked through the neighborhood, one of its community watch leaders, twenty-eight-year-old George Zimmerman, spotted him from his car. Zimmerman called the police, reporting Martin as suspicious.

Zimmerman abruptly broke off his conversation with the police dispatcher, claiming that Martin had started running. He brought a handgun as he gave chase. While the exact details about what happened next remain unclear, the two men clashed violently, leaving Zimmerman bloodied. As Martin left the scene, heading toward the town house where he was staying, Zimmerman raised his weapon and fired. The shot struck and killed Martin.

News of the exchange and Zimmerman's arrest made national headlines. He claimed that he had fired in self-defense, citing Florida's stand-your-ground law. This legislation gives a person the right to shoot and kill another person in self-defense, even if it would have been possible to flee the situation safely. Many Americans felt that the shooting was racially motivated. (Martin was black. Zimmerman has been described as white, Hispanic, or both.) A jury sided with Zimmerman. It found that he had fired legally in self-defense, and he was cleared of all charges.

Artist Tatyana Fazlalizadeh attends the 2018 unveiling of her mural portrait of Trayvon Martin in New York City.

under siege as long as I'm your president." While gun-control law did not change at the federal level, some states beefed up their gun restrictions.

As the debate escalated, the two sides rallied around their long-held positions. Those who opposed new gun laws argued that mass shootings were a mental health issue, not a gun issue. They said that the focus should be on health care and terrorism, not on restricting gun rights. However, those calling for greater gun restrictions insisted that the problem was on both fronts. It wasn't just a mental health issue. It was also a gun issue. Many Democrats worked to propose further gun restrictions, but the Republican-controlled Congress and White House blocked the way.

President Donald Trump spoke at the annual NRA meeting in May 2018. There, he spoke of his support of the NRA mission to ensure gun rights in the United States.

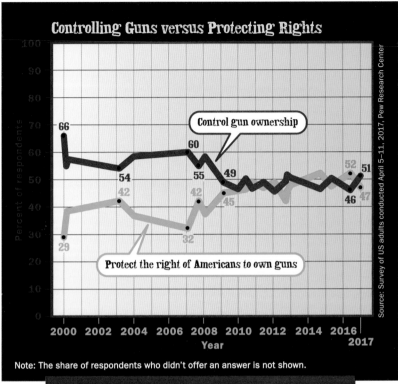

Controlling Guns versus Protecting Rights

Control gun ownership

Protect the right of Americans to own guns

Note: The share of respondents who didn't offer an answer is not shown.

Source: Survey of US adults conducted April 5–11, 2017, Pew Research Center

Polls show that in the first two decades of the twenty-first century, the divide between Americans who want laws to control gun ownership and those who want to protect the right to own guns has narrowed significantly.

The debate rages on. Gun control continues to divide Americans. Where should the government draw the line between individual rights and the safety of society? The question has divided the nation, and it's not going away anytime soon.

Chapter 3

A QUESTION OF SAFETY

On November 5, 2017, twenty-six-year-old Devin Patrick Kelley entered First Baptist Church in Sutherland Springs, Texas. The church was filled for a regular Sunday service. But Kelley was not there to join in on song and prayer. As he stepped through the church doors, he wore a black face mask and carried a Ruger AR-556 semiautomatic rifle. The self-loading weapon was capable of firing a single round with every squeeze of the trigger, in very rapid succession.

Kelley shouted vulgar profanity at the churchgoers and then began to fire. He emptied about thirty magazines (a device that stores and feeds ammunition into a weapon). Each magazine held fifteen rounds. No one in the church had a chance.

Fifty-five-year-old Sutherland Springs resident Stephen Willeford lived half a block from the church. When his daughter told him what was happening there, Willeford sprang into action. The former NRA firearms instructor grabbed his gun and rushed to the scene. He didn't even stop to put on shoes.

Stephen Willeford attends a memorial service in November 2017 after a deadly shooting at the First Baptist Church of Sutherland Springs in Texas. Willeford and fellow citizen Johnnie Langendorff chased down the gunman.

When Willeford arrived, Kelley was near the exit of the church. Willeford took cover behind a parked pickup truck and fired at Kelley. At least one of his shots struck Kelley, who was wearing a bulletproof vest. Kelley jumped into his truck and sped away from the scene. At that moment, another citizen, Johnnie Langendorff, was watching the scene play out from his own truck. Willeford hopped into the truck with Langendorff, and they took off in pursuit. After several minutes of the high-speed chase, Kelley crashed his truck. Soon after, he killed himself.

Americans hailed Willeford as a national hero. He at first avoided public attention for his actions. Gun-rights supporters said that as a private gun owner, he had saved countless lives. He was the perfect example, they said, of how gun rights protect people more than they endanger them. Willeford agreed, writing later, "Anti-gun politicians and anti-gun activists have made clear their belief that the way to stop criminals is to restrict the rights of law-abiding citizens, and many have blamed the men and women of the NRA for acts of deranged individuals. . . . Sometimes, it feels like the mainstream media hates firearms. I am proof that they are wrong. I am also proof that . . . the best way to stop a bad guy with a gun is a good guy with a gun."

Willeford's opinion drove to the heart of the gun debate. Is society safer because people like him have access to guns? Or is it more dangerous because people like Kelley have equal access?

DO GUNS PROTECT US OR ENDANGER US?

The Sutherland Springs shooting and others like it raise complicated issues. Some Americans say that lax gun laws allowed a dangerous man, Kelley, to obtain a powerful semiautomatic weapon and use it on innocent people. Gun-control advocates say that such shootings prove that the United States needs stricter gun control.

Gun-rights supporters point to Willeford's actions. Willeford was a law-abiding citizen who exercised his Second Amendment right to keep and bear arms. Gun-rights supporters say that his story shows why it is so important to protect the gun rights of ordinary citizens. If he hadn't responded, gun in hand, how much worse might the situation have been?

The arguments for and against gun control often revolve around one central question: Do guns in society make citizens safer or put them in danger? Those who favor stricter gun control often claim that inadequate gun regulation makes the United States a dangerous place. They point to western Europe as proof. Western Europe is culturally and economically similar to the United States. Most western European countries have stricter gun laws, so their societies have far fewer guns per person than the United States has. Their rates of shooting deaths—both intentional and accidental—are also much lower. According to the Centers for Disease Control and Prevention, from 1999 to 2016, more than twenty-six thousand children under the age of eighteen died as a result of firearms. That figure accounts for 91 percent of the global total among wealthy nations, most of which have more stringent gun-control laws.

Gun-control supporters argue that limiting the number of guns in society also limits the number of gun deaths that occur. When criminals and potential criminals have a harder time getting guns, everyone is safer. When children do not have easy access to firearms, accidental shootings decrease.

"The U.S., which has the most firearms per capita in the world, suffers disproportionately from firearms compared with other high-income countries. These results are consistent with the hypothesis that our firearms are killing us rather than protecting us."
—Erin Grinshteyn, professor and coauthor of a gun violence study, *American Journal of Medicine,* 2016

Those who favor less gun control argue that law-abiding citizens with guns can prevent crime. When adults own guns, they can defend themselves and others from criminal attacks. Criminals must then consider the possibility of running into gun-wielding citizens, which theoretically reduces crime. And an armed citizenry provides the nation with a collective defense against tyranny, they say. Gun-rights proponents point out that in the American Revolution, armed citizens helped secure personal freedom for all.

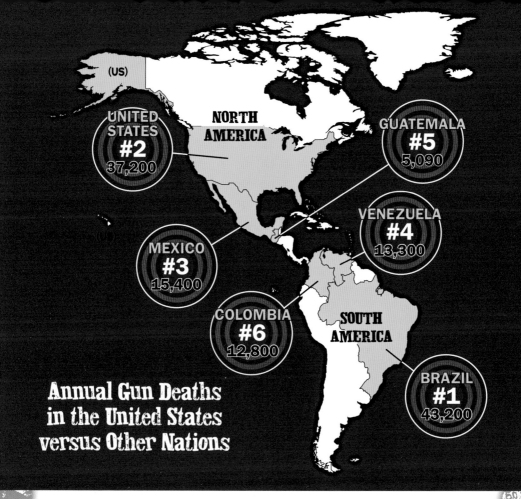

Annual Gun Deaths in the United States versus Other Nations

(US)

NORTH AMERICA

UNITED STATES
#2
37,200

GUATEMALA
#5
5,090

VENEZUELA
#4
13,300

MEXICO
#3
15,400

COLOMBIA
#6
12,800

SOUTH AMERICA

BRAZIL
#1
43,200

Some gun-rights activists point to Mexico's experience as proof that excessive gun control doesn't work. Mexico's stricter gun laws are designed to prevent drug traffickers and other criminals from arming themselves. But these criminals are heavily armed despite the laws. Critics say that the restrictions keep guns only from law-abiding citizens and do little to stop criminals from stockpiling them.

Meanwhile, gun-control supporters note that Mexican gun laws don't work because US gun laws are so lax. From 2009 until 2018, about 70 percent of the guns recovered and traced in Mexico came from the United States. It's hard to buy a gun

EUROPE

ASIA

AFRICA

AUSTRALIA

6 countries, combined, make up 126,000 gun deaths (50.4% approx.).

193 countries, combined, make up 124,000 gun deaths (49.6% approx.).

Source: Institute for Health Metrics and Evaluation

legally in Mexico. But it's easy to buy an illegal gun smuggled in from the United States. "Every year, thousands of weapons and millions of US dollars in cash enter illegally into Mexico from the north, strengthening the cartels and other criminal organizations that create violence in Mexico," Mexico's then president Enrique Peña Nieto said in 2016.

ACCIDENTAL SHOOTINGS

Criminal use of guns isn't the only danger of firearms. Many gun-related deaths are accidents. A child may find an adult's loaded gun, take it out to play, and accidentally trigger it.

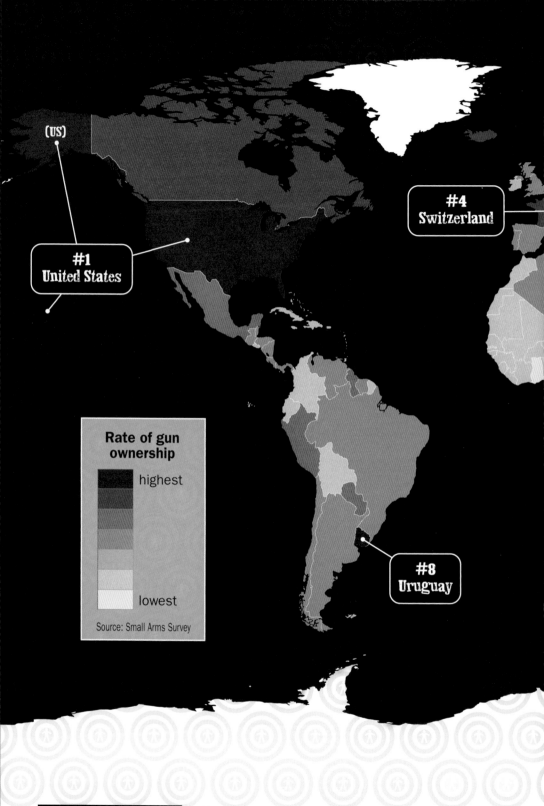

(US)

#4
Switzerland

#1
United States

Rate of gun ownership

highest

lowest

Source: Small Arms Survey

#8
Uruguay

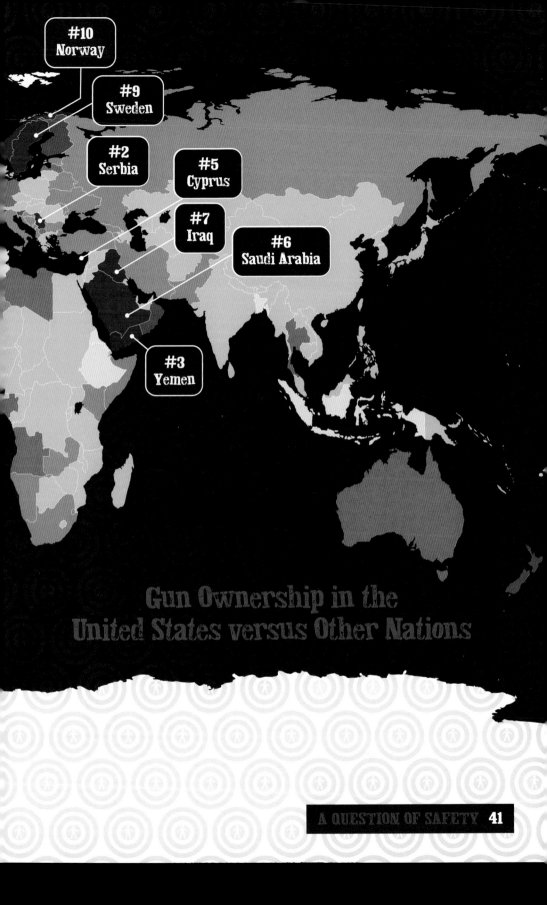

#10
Norway

#9
Sweden

#2
Serbia

#5
Cyprus

#7
Iraq

#6
Saudi Arabia

#3
Yemen

Gun Ownership in the
United States versus Other Nations

A hunter may mistake another hunter for prey, accidentally fire a gun in the wrong direction, or injure someone with a stray bullet. Irresponsible teenagers may goof off with guns without understanding and respecting the very real danger they represent.

Firearms education and gun-safety classes can curb irresponsible adult gun use. But US children still face a great risk of accidental shooting. A 2018 study published in the *Journal of Urban Health* estimated that about 4.6 million children in the United States live in homes with loaded, unlocked guns. Research published in the *Annals of Internal Medicine* in 2014 shows that access to guns doubles the risk of homicide and triples the risk of suicide.

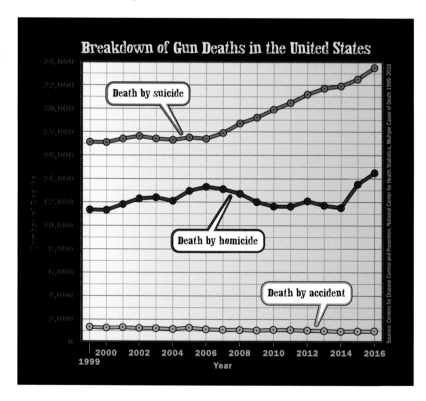

Breakdown of Gun Deaths in the United States

Death by suicide

Death by homicide

Death by accident

Sources: Centers for Disease Control and Prevention, National Center for Health Statistics, Multiple Cause of Death 1999-2016

Gun companies, fearing liability (legal financial responsibility) for such accidents, have programs that give away millions of free gunlocks. Industry trade organizations launched Project ChildSafe, a program that offers free kits by mail. Gun owners can also get locks from programs that cities, police departments, and community organizations run. When engaged, the small devices prevent guns from firing, even when they are loaded.

Yet even with these measures, many children still have access to guns. And how far should government go to protect them? Some gun-control advocates think that gunlocks should be mandatory. Others suggest that laws should require technology that allows only a gun's owner to operate it.

The NRA and other gun-rights groups support the use of gunlocks and other safety devices, but they believe they should be voluntary. They say that laws forcing gun owners to use safety devices are a needless government intrusion into people's private lives.

DOMESTIC VIOLENCE

Gun violence against women, particularly during domestic abuse, is higher in the United States than it is in other wealthy nations. Millions of women suffer from domestic violence in the home, and when their attacker has a gun, abuse can turn into murder. According to Everytown for Gun Safety, a group that supports gun control, the presence of a gun during domestic violence increases the likelihood of murder by a factor of five. Abusers may also use guns to threaten and coerce their victims.

Gun-control supporters generally favor laws that keep guns out of the hands of people convicted of domestic abuse. They argue that anyone with a history of such violent behavior presents a grave threat to the people who live with them.

Gun-rights supporters counter that such laws are too sweeping and that they would infringe upon the Second Amendment rights of too many people.

SUICIDES

According to the Centers for Disease Control and Prevention, more than half of all suicides in the United States are gun suicides. Suicide is the third-leading cause of death in the United States among teenagers, accounting for 11 percent of teen deaths. Only accidents (48 percent) and homicides (13 percent) account for more deaths. The teen brain is not fully developed, so teens are more easily overcome by depression and impulsiveness than are emotionally mature adults.

Most suicide attempts are unsuccessful. Drug overdose is the most common method of attempted suicide, and this method fails about 97 percent of the time. Suicide attempts involving firearms are a different story. According to the San Francisco, California-based Giffords Law Center to Prevent Gun Violence, guns are used in only about 5 percent of suicide attempts. But they are responsible for about 50 percent of suicide deaths, says the center, whose mission is to research gun violence in the United States and promote laws to reduce it. (The center is named for former US representative Gabrielle Giffords, a victim of gun violence in 2011.) Those who turn to firearms in a suicidal moment of helplessness and desperation are highly unlikely to survive the attempt. Further, studies show that suicide rates for adolescents who live in homes with guns are far higher than for those who live in homes without guns. The risk rate increases anywhere from twice to ten times, depending on factors such as age and gun storage methods. Researchers have concluded that suicide success rates correlate directly with access to firearms.

Suicide attempts are usually rash and impulsive. According to a study conducted by the Centers for Disease Control and Prevention, 24 percent of people who attempt suicide take less than five minutes to make their decision and 70 percent take less than one hour. David Hemenway, director of the Injury Control Research Center with the Harvard School of Public Health, says that failed suicide attempts don't necessarily lead to repeat attempts. "Studies show that most attempters act on impulse, in moments of panic or despair," he said. "Once the acute feelings ease, 90 percent do not go on to die by suicide."

However, people who use guns to attempt suicide hardly ever get a second chance. Many believe the United States needs tighter gun control to keep guns away from suicide-prone juveniles. And gun-purchase waiting periods can reduce

Former US representative Gabrielle Giffords was shot during a political appearance in Arizona in 2011. She and her husband are active gun-control advocates. They founded what eventually became the Giffords Law Center to Prevent Gun Violence.

impulsive suicidal behavior in adults. The story of twenty-seven-year-old Kerry Lewiecki illustrates this. In 2010 Lewiecki was a law school graduate who was planning to marry his longtime girlfriend in a few months. Those who knew him don't know why, but Lewiecki walked into a store in Oregon—a state with no waiting period—and bought a gun. He used it to kill himself that day. It was a rash and impulsive act that a waiting period would likely have prevented.

Gun-rights supporters argue that guns are not the cause of suicides but merely tools used in committing suicide. Even if guns are not accessible, determined individuals have many other options for taking their own lives. Opponents of gun control further argue that law-abiding citizens should not have to give up gun rights to protect potential suicide victims.

SELF-DEFENSE

According to a 2017 Pew Research Center study, gun owners cite five main reasons for owning guns: protection against crime (self-defense), hunting, sport shooting, collecting, and job-related. The reason cited most often is self-defense. A gun can theoretically level the playing field between criminals and their potential victims. A homeowner with a gun can fend off a robber. An armed woman walking alone can use her gun to repel an attacker. She may not even have to fire the gun for it to be effective. Just having it may be enough of a deterrent.

The number of defensive gun uses in the United States is hard to pin down. Gun-rights groups claim more than two million defensive gun uses in the United States every year. This statistic is based on polling data in which respondents volunteer information about their own behavior. Gun-control advocates say that the polling data is unreliable and that the real number is far lower.

Heavily armed guards at Trump Tower in New York City carry weapons as part of their job. The building is the headquarters of the many businesses that President Trump owns.

The use of guns for self-defense is actually quite rare. According to a study by the Violence Policy Center, from 2014 to 2016, only about 1 percent of victims of violent crimes used—or attempted to use—a gun in self-defense. "Guns are far more likely to be used in a homicide than in a justifiable homicide by a private citizen," said Josh Sugarmann, director of the center. "In fact, a gun is far more likely to be stolen than used in self-defense."

Gun-control advocates point to this number as proof that Americans rarely use guns in self-defense. Meanwhile, gun-rights supporters argue the opposite. They say that in

"The average person . . . has basically no chance in their lifetime ever to use a gun in self-defense. But . . . every day, they have a chance to use the gun inappropriately. They have a chance, they get angry. They get scared."
—David Hemenway, Harvard researcher, 2018

many cases, when a citizen draws a weapon in self-defense, that person prevents a violent crime—and the incident goes unreported. Therefore, many gun-rights supporters reject the usefulness of the center's data.

Some Americans wonder whether guns owned for self-defense do more harm than good. A 2009 University of Pennsylvania study found that a person carrying a gun is 4.5 times more likely to be shot than a person who does not carry one. Victims actively trying to use a gun for self-defense are still more likely to be shot. Gun-control advocates argue that guns provide a false sense of security while raising the risk of death or serious injury. Gun-rights activists counter that many people carry guns because they are already at a higher risk for violence. This, they say, skews the numbers. It invalidates the argument that carrying a gun in self-defense does more harm than good.

The use of firearms in self-defense brings up a related question: When is it acceptable to shoot at another human being? Most people agree that if a criminal poses an immediate threat to someone's life, extreme force is justified. But few incidents are so clear-cut. What about an unarmed burglar in a person's home? Or someone vandalizing private property? Where do we draw the line between acceptable self-defense and unacceptable overkill? What responsibility does a citizen have to avoid a potentially lethal exchange? The question also extends to law enforcement. When is it okay for a police officer to use lethal force? Are police obligated to use the same set of rules as civilians?

Americans grappling with these questions fall into two main camps. One is the stand-your-ground camp. They believe that a person under threat has the right to stand their ground and fire at the offender. The other camp takes a "duty to retreat" approach. Those in this camp believe that people under threat must make every effort to remove themselves from the situation before firing. Only when all other options have failed should someone open fire on an attacker.

US laws on self-defensive gun use differ from state to state. However, most state laws contain some form of the following principle: a person who faces immediate danger from another person may use the *minimum* necessary force to secure his or her own safety. Individual states have unique exceptions and restrictions to the rule, but that's the backbone of most self-defense gun laws.

What is the minimum necessary force? It's just enough force to prevent injury to yourself or someone you wish to protect, but no more. For example, if a mugger comes at

CASTLE LAWS

Many US states have laws that permit residents to defend themselves from intruders in their homes. These castle doctrine laws, or castle laws, are based on the idea that people have the right to defend their "castles" (their homes) and innocent people in them from illegal trespassing or violent attack.

Castle laws are unique in that they generally ignore the rule of minimum necessary force. They give citizens broad protection from criminal charges and civil lawsuits for using self-defensive violent force in their own homes. While most people support the general principle of castle laws, some argue that they go too far, excusing unnecessary excessive force.

Most states have castle laws, but they vary from state to state. In some states, homeowners must verbally announce their intent to shoot before doing so, giving an intruder a chance to flee. Other states require no such warning. Some states provide the legal protection of a castle law no matter where the person feels threatened. Florida law, for example, provides the legal protection of a castle law to people anywhere they legally are allowed to be—even in public places.

FLORIDA'S STAND-YOUR-GROUND LAW

In 2018 two Florida men got into a shoving match over a parking spot. After a brief scuffle, twenty-eight-year-old Markeis McGlockton began to walk away from the fight. It could have ended there. But instead, Michael Drejka, who McGlockton had pushed to the ground, drew his gun, aimed, and fired. The shot killed McGlockton.

The shooting sparked outrage, especially when officials initially chose not to charge Drejka in the shooting. Eventually, Drejka was arrested and charged with manslaughter (unlawful killing not based on intent to harm or kill). The shooting threw Florida's broad stand-your-ground law into the national spotlight.

This wasn't the first time the Florida law had come under fire. It was at the heart of the high-profile trial of George Zimmerman, who claimed self-defense in shooting and killing teenager Trayvon Martin in 2012. The Florida law, which has no element of duty to retreat, requires only that a shooter feel threatened to warrant defensive gun use. Critics argue that the law sets a shoot first, ask questions later standard. In the Trayvon Martin case, the jury found Zimmerman not guilty.

Stand-Your-Ground and Duty-to-Retreat Laws

● States that have stand-your-ground laws without the duty-to-retreat exemption

● States that have stand-your-ground laws with the duty-to-retreat exemption

Source: FindLaw.com, 2018

you with a baseball bat, you could argue that firing a gun at that person is a reasonable level of force. However, if you shoot the mugger and knock them to the ground, firing additional shots would be unnecessary. You could face charges for the additional shooting for exceeding the minimum necessary force.

Technically, a person who shoots someone in self-defense may be arrested and called before a judge. The shooter must demonstrate how their actions were necessary for self-defense. If the judge finds that the shooter used more than the minimum necessary force, the shooter could face a criminal trial. In practice, however, the US justice system rarely prosecutes civilians in self-defense cases. The courts generally give citizens the very broad benefit of the doubt.

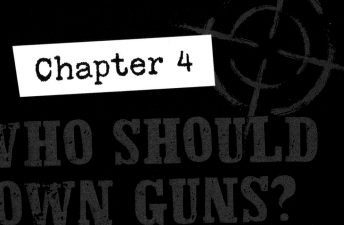

Chapter 4

WHO SHOULD OWN GUNS?

In 2010 a new version of an old debate erupted in the US Congress and on the national political stage. Americans were divided over who should be allowed to own and carry guns in the United States. The basic issue was nothing new. But the specifics made people—even staunch gun-rights supporters—a little uneasy.

The question seemed simple: Should suspected terrorists have the right to own and carry weapons? The question arose from an FBI study that found that from 2004 to 2010, more than eleven hundred suspected terrorists had legally bought firearms or explosives in the United States. US laws already prevented suspected terrorists from boarding commercial airplanes. Airlines could not accept passengers whose names appeared on a national No Fly List (part of the FBI's Terrorist Watch List). But many people on the No Fly List could still buy firearms—as long as they weren't convicted felons or illegal immigrants. Many members of Congress wanted to change

A TSA (Transportation Security Administration) agent talks with a traveler as she does a weapons security check at the international airport in Denver, Colorado. Passengers have the right to request a pat down instead of going through a scanning machine.

that. They wanted to add suspected terrorists to the list of people who cannot legally buy firearms in the United States.

The Gun Control Act of 1968 makes it illegal for certain categories of people in the United States to own guns:

- people convicted in federal courts of crimes punishable by imprisonment for more than one year;
- people convicted in state courts of crimes punishable by imprisonment for more than two years;
- fugitives from justice;
- people who are unlawful users of or are addicted to drugs;

- people who have been declared in court as having a mental defect (an illness or a neurological deficiency) or who have been committed to mental institutions;
- people illegally or unlawfully in the country, as well as visitors to the United States, unless they possess a current valid hunting license;
- people dishonorably discharged from the US armed forces;
- people who have renounced (given up) their US citizenship;
- people subject to restraining orders (court orders preventing them from harassing, stalking, or threatening others); and
- people convicted of domestic violence.

Keeping guns away from terrorists may seem like a no-brainer. Terrorists endanger all of society. Many of them kill indiscriminately, without careful selection of victims, and without remorse. But the matter isn't that simple. Some people end up on a watch list by mistake. Others on the FBI's Terrorist Watch List have not committed any serious crimes. The FBI merely suspects these people of being terrorists or of having close ties to terrorists. Critics also say that Muslims are most likely to end up on watch lists. They ask, Can the government deny an individual's Second Amendment rights based solely on suspicion? And if so, can the government rely on factors such as race, religion, and ethnic background to make these determinations?

In 2010 the US Senate held a committee meeting to discuss proposed legislation that would add suspected terrorists to the list of people prohibited from owning guns. The heated debate left people on all side conflicted. The majority of Democrats, who had sponsored the bill, felt it was a reasonable step to take. "This is a homeland security issue, not a gun issue," said Democrat Frank Lautenberg of New Jersey. "There's no reason we shouldn't be able to stop a terrorist from buying a dangerous weapon in the United States."

The committee invited New York City's Republican mayor, Michael Bloomberg, to speak. Republicans generally favor protection of gun rights. But Bloomberg, as the mayor of a large city struggling with gun violence, had founded Everytown for Gun Safety in 2006. About the proposed new law, he said, "If society decides that these people are too dangerous to get on an airplane with other people, then it's probably appropriate to look very hard before you let them buy a gun."

South Carolina senator Lindsey Graham, also a Republican, countered, "But we're talking about a constitutional right here."

Another Republican, Maine senator Susan Collins, pointed out that "the watch list can be inaccurate." She added, "It is not . . . the equivalent of a criminal history report." So being on the list does not necessarily mean a person has actually done anything wrong.

Since 2010 the NRA has almost exclusively supported Republican points of view, which include being tough on terror. But in this case, NRA officials denounced the proposal as a sneaky plan to undermine the Second Amendment. They argued that, under the law, the government would have the legal right to place names on the list without oversight, snuffing out Second Amendment rights. The NRA considered the proposal unconstitutional, and some members of Congress agreed. They thought the plan would set a dangerous precedent. Two more bills, sponsored by Democrats, to limit suspected terrorists from buying guns were introduced—and

"If you are considered to be too dangerous to fly on an airplane, you should not be able to buy a firearm. This bill [to stop suspected terrorists from buying firearms] is a sensible step we can take right now to reform our nation's gun laws while protecting the Second Amendment rights of law-abiding Americans."
—Republican senator Susan Collins of Maine, 2018

failed—in 2015. Another new bill, introduced in 2018, would bar people on the No Fly List from buying firearms. However, it appears unlikely to pass, given the Republican-controlled US Senate and the lack of NRA support.

INDIVIDUAL VERSUS COLLECTIVE GUN RIGHTS

The Second Amendment shows clearly that the founders of the United States intended private gun ownership to be legal in the United States. But did they really mean it to be an absolute right of all Americans? Scholars, lawyers, and judges study and interpret the Constitution in different ways. Some want to focus on preserving the intentions of the nation's founders in the laws of the modern era. Others believe that the Constitution is a flexible document that allows for changing interpretations. What was true in the eighteenth century, for example, may no longer be widely accepted in the twenty-first century. But whatever the founders' intentions, most Americans agree that young children and violent criminals should not have guns. Americans disagree over the gun rights of other groups and where to draw the line.

The answer to this question depends on how a person interprets the Second Amendment. Many believe it grants the American citizenry, as a collective group, the right to keep and bear arms. They think the founders meant that society has the right—even the obligation—to own and use guns for defense. Supporters of this idea point to the situation of the young nation. The United States had little money. It could not afford to maintain a standing army. Foreign powers ruled the lands to the north, west, and south. American Indians and European settlers were in violent conflict over control of land. Given these realities, the founders wanted to ensure that the federal government could call upon local militias for national defense. In the preamble to the Second Amendment, the founders specifically mentioned the role of militias in national security. And, the argument goes, they couldn't have meant to guarantee individual gun rights because in that era, many Americans had no such rights. Slaves couldn't own guns, and law enforcement was quick to disarm violent criminals. Whatever the founders had in mind, the absolute right of individuals to own a gun doesn't appear to have been the intent.

Other Americans interpret the Second Amendment differently. They focus on the wording about the right of the people (as individuals) to keep and bear arms, rather than on maintaining a militia for the collective good. In this analysis, just as the First Amendment grants all individuals the right of free speech, so the Second Amendment grants all individuals the right of gun ownership. If the government passes a law that prevents a citizen from owning guns, that law violates the Constitution.

The issue of collective versus individual rights was at the heart of the 2008 US Supreme Court case *District of Columbia v. Heller*. The court ruled 5–4 that the Second Amendment grants individual gun rights. Explaining the court's decision, Justice Antonin Scalia wrote, "Nowhere else in the Constitution does a 'right' attributed to 'the people' refer to anything other than an individual right. What is more, in all six other provisions of the Constitution that mention 'the people,' the

Dick Heller (*center*), the plaintiff in the US Supreme Court case *District of Columbia v. Heller*, flashes the victory sign after picking up his gun registration in August 2008. The case challenged the ban on handguns in Washington, DC.

term unambiguously [clearly] refers to all members of the political community, not an unspecified subset."

Still, the verdict was not unanimous. Justice John Paul Stevens wrote one of the dissenting opinions. He described why he disagreed with the ruling. "The Second Amendment was adopted to protect the right of the people of each of the several States to maintain a well-regulated militia," Stevens wrote. He continued,

> It was a response to concerns raised during the ratification of the Constitution that the power of Congress to disarm the state militias and create a national standing army posed an intolerable threat to the sovereignty of the several States. Neither the text of the Amendment nor the arguments advanced by its proponents evidenced the slightest interest in limiting any legislature's

authority to regulate private civilian uses of firearms. Specifically, there is no indication that the Framers of the Amendment intended to enshrine the common-law [law that comes from past custom rather than formal statutes] right of self-defense in the Constitution.

So Stevens was saying that the founders had little interest in guaranteeing the rights of every citizen to own guns but rather were interested in protecting the nation as a whole.

CRIMINALS

Regardless of whether the right to keep and bear arms is an individual right or a collective right, US law prevents people convicted of felonies from owning guns and ammunition. Neither can a person convicted of misdemeanor domestic battery. (Domestic battery is violence against a person with whom one shares a close relationship, such as a family member, roommate, friend, spouse, girlfriend, or boyfriend.) Individual states can restore this right in special cases. But most felons face severe penalties (up to ten years in prison) if caught with firearms, even at home.

Even these restrictions are a source of controversy. Some ex-criminals who have served their time and are rehabilitated (restored to a positive and useful place in society) argue that the restrictions unfairly deny them their constitutional rights. Some law-abiding citizens agree. They see the criminal restrictions as a slippery slope leading toward more unfair restrictions. They point out that the Second Amendment says nothing about denying criminals the right to bear arms. Rather, the amendment guarantees this right for *all* people. Furthermore, say gun-rights advocates, the law doesn't distinguish between different types of felonies. Felonies are not all the same, and they pose different levels of danger to society. For example, tax evasion (illegally avoiding tax payment) is a felony. But since it is a nonviolent felony, some people believe this crime should not lead to the loss of Second Amendment rights.

Other people point to Americans who have been convicted of a felony crime in a foreign country, where laws are different from those in the United States. They also point to those convicted in a country without due process of law (a legal system of fairly and systematically determining a person's innocence or guilt). These people, if they come back to the United States, would automatically lose their gun rights. Is that fair and constitutional?

Many gun-control advocates feel that protecting the rights of convicted criminals is far less important than protecting the safety of society. They argue that felons and people convicted of domestic abuse should never have access to firearms. By committing these types of crimes, these people forfeit a variety of rights. For example, convicted felons may also lose the right to vote, hold office, or live in federally funded housing. Gun-control advocates say that losing the right to own guns is just part of the price criminals must pay for their crimes.

> "I can only assume that firearms in a 'gun-free' America would be just as prevalent as illegal drugs are today or alcohol was during the prohibition. In both cases, drugs and alcohol are readily available and the laws banning them have created entire criminal enterprises. Ban guns and I'll let you know who will still have them: criminals."
>
> —Ryan M. Cleckner, author and firearms industry executive, 2017

MENTAL ILLNESS

Similar laws restrict gun ownership for individuals who have been legally declared to be mentally deficient (having intelligence or mental function well below normal). People who have been committed to psychiatric institutions are not allowed to own guns either. These laws are meant to keep guns away from people who lack the mental capacity or emotional stability to use a gun responsibly. The laws also apply to people who have psychological disorders that could cause them to act in antisocial ways or without fully understanding the consequences of their actions. For example, a court may rule that a person with a mental illness such as schizophrenia (a condition in which a person has difficulty distinguishing reality from the imaginary) is too unpredictable to safely own a firearm.

But denying gun rights for psychiatric reasons is difficult to carry out. Psychiatric institutions do not consistently report committals to local authorities, as the law requires. And states do not usually have enough staff or money to make sure they do a better job. Many people with psychiatric conditions who, by law, should be denied firearms have sailed through background checks. And some experts argue that requiring health-care professionals to report a person's mental condition raises serious concerns about the privacy rights of mentally ill patients. Furthermore, in many cases, very little data is available to make a strong link between mental illness or deficiency and a tendency toward gun violence.

Guns and mental illness were at the forefront of the gun-control debate in 2018, after the Parkland, Florida, school shooting. Although he had no formal diagnosis of mental illness, the nineteen-year-old shooter at the school had a history of troubling behavior, including violent behavior and cruelty to animals. Two weeks after the shooting, Trump spoke on television about taking guns away from the mentally ill without getting court approval first. "I like taking the guns early, like in this crazy man's case that just took place in [Parkland] Florida," he said. "To go to court would have taken a long time. Take the guns first, go through due process second."

Trump's comment started a storm of debate—from both gun-rights advocates and proponents of gun control. Trump's intention—keeping guns out of the hands of dangerous people—may have been legitimate. But his suggestion to avoid due process horrified many Americans. His idea of doing so is at the core of what gun-rights advocates fear: government taking guns from law-abiding citizens. And many mental health experts say that the vast majority of people

GUNS AND DEMENTIA

In 2015 a dispatcher in Dalles, Oregon, received an emergency 911 call. "My husband accidentally shot me," reported seventy-five-year-old Dee Hill.

As she made the call, her husband, Darrell Hill, sat in his wheelchair near his wife—unaware of what had just happened. He was a former police chief and sheriff who had been around guns all of his life. But he suffered from rapidly progressive dementia. It robbed him of much of his intellect and memory, as well as his ability to engage with the world.

According to a 2017 Pew Research study, 9 percent of Americans sixty-five years and older are living with some form of dementia. And almost half of them are gun owners. If people with mental illness cannot legally own guns, what about people living with dementia? It's a difficult problem to address, and it's made worse by a general lack of data about guns and people with dementia. Gun-control supporters argue that the NRA uses its wide-ranging political power to discourage research into this and other gun-control topics.

Dee Hill's story didn't end with the shooting. She survived the gunshot after almost two months in the hospital. But much is unknown about the relationship between gun violence and people with impaired memory.

with mental disorders do not resort to gun violence much less mass shootings. They say that linking mental illness to mass violence is a distraction from the real problems that mentally ill people face and that drive killers to their actions. And it shows why even an idea that almost everyone is behind in theory can be so difficult to put into action.

YOUTH AND GUNS

In the United States, minors usually are legally defined as Americans under eighteen. They do not have the same constitutional rights that adults have. Kids can't vote or buy alcohol. Their driving and employment privileges are limited. And, according to federal law, minors can't buy firearms and ammunition. People under twenty-one can't buy handguns and handgun-only ammunition. However, minors may own some guns with parental permission.

The reasons for restricting youth gun rights are straightforward. Young people generally lack the knowledge and judgment to operate a firearm safely. And the rate of accidental shooting deaths among youth is far higher than it is among adults. In a five-year study (2005–2010) by the Giffords Law Center to Prevent Gun Violence, data

In 2012 Lucy McBath's seventeen-year-old son was shot and killed in an argument about loud music at a gas station in Atlanta, Georgia. After his death, she became a vocal gun-control advocate and was elected to the US House of Representatives in 2018.

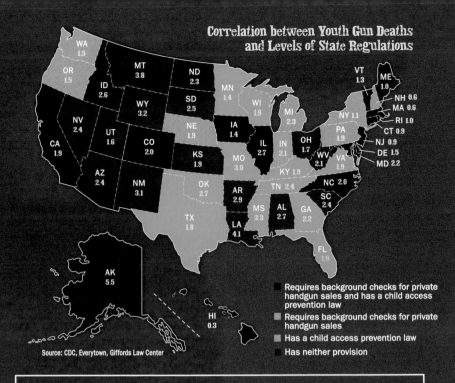

Correlation between Youth Gun Deaths and Levels of State Regulations

WA 1.5	
OR 1.5	
MT 3.8	
ND 2.3	
ID 2.6	
MN 1.4	
VT 1.3	
ME 1.0	
NH 0.6	
WY 3.2	
SD 2.5	
WI 1.9	
MA 0.6	
NV 2.4	
NE 1.9	
MI 2.3	
NY 1.1	
RI 1.0	
UT 1.6	
IA 1.4	
PA 1.9	
CT 0.9	
CA 1.9	
CO 2.0	
IL 2.7	
IN 2.1	
OH 1.7	
NJ 0.9	
KS 1.9	
MO 3.0	
WV 2.1	
VA 1.9	
DE 1.5	
AZ 2.4	
NM 3.1	
KY 1.9	
MD 2.2	
OK 2.7	
AR 2.9	
TN 2.4	
NC 2.0	
SC 2.4	
TX 1.8	
MS 3.3	
AL 2.7	
GA 2.2	
LA 4.1	
FL 1.9	
AK 5.5	
HI 0.3	

Legend:
- Requires background checks for private handgun sales and has a child access prevention law
- Requires background checks for private handgun sales
- Has a child access prevention law
- Has neither provision

Source: CDC, Everytown, Giffords Law Center

Generally speaking, research shows that states with the fewest regulations controlling youth access to guns have higher rates of gun deaths among young people. This infographic shows data collected between 1999 and 2016, the most recent year for which the data is available.

showed that almost thirty-eight hundred Americans died from unintentional shootings. More than thirteen hundred of those victims were under twenty-five years old.

Young people are less likely to understand the full consequences of their actions. Because they are still developing intellectual and emotional maturity, they are more likely to act rashly with guns. And young people who commit violent crimes are much more likely to do so again. Still, many minors do own guns—with their parents' permission—and know how to use them safely. According to the Pew Research Center, 37 percent of gun owners report that they were younger than eighteen when they first owned a gun. Hunting is a way of life for many families in rural areas. Young people in these families learn the proper handling of weapons from their parents and other responsible adults. Many states require minors to pass gun safety classes before using weapons legally.

The desire to keep guns out of the hands of children is shared by both gun-control and gun-rights advocates. But the two camps disagree on methods. Many gun-rights supporters think that state or parental control is best. Gun-control supporters often favor more federal control and stricter penalties for those caught providing firearms illegally to children.

ARE GUN COMPANIES RESPONSIBLE?

Some gun-control activists believe that gun manufacturers and dealers should be liable for damages that come from gun crimes or gun accidents. They believe that the success of similar lawsuits against other companies, especially tobacco companies, justifies this. In 1998, for example, forty-six states sued major tobacco companies—and won—for knowingly selling products that cause cancer and other serious health problems.

Gun-control activists believe that a company should be accountable in state and federal courts if its product endangers consumers. Gun companies and gun-rights activists oppose such lawsuits. They argue that as long as manufacturers and dealers sell their guns legally, they bear no responsibility for the actions of buyers. In 2005 the US Congress passed the Protection of Lawful Commerce in Arms Act. This law shields gun manufacturers and dealers from most civil lawsuits as long as they have sold guns legally and with no knowledge of a buyer's intent. The protections under this law are not absolute. The law includes several exemptions to protection, including when firearms are knowingly sold for criminal intent or in violation of state or federal law. Opponents have legally challenged the act several times but failed. Furthermore, many states have their own blanket immunity laws, which protect gun manufacturers and dealers from liability and essentially render the federal law irrelevant. However in March 2019, Connecticut's supreme court ruled that the families of nine victims of the Sandy Hook school shootings could sue Remington Arms, the manufacturer of the rifle used in the shooting.

Chapter 5

ARE ALL FIREARMS CREATED EQUAL?

Shots rang out at the Tree of Life Jewish synagogue in Pittsburgh, Pennsylvania, on October 27, 2018. A forty-six-year-old man had entered the place of worship and opened fire. His shooting rampage left eleven people dead before police finally captured and arrested him.

It was a shocking hate crime. But the killer's choice of weapon did not shock experts. It was a Colt AR-15, a semiautomatic version of the M16 military rifle. The weapon was all too familiar to those investigating mass shootings in the United States—and around the world. The AR-15's low cost, ease of use, and ability to fire three rounds with a single squeeze of the trigger has made it the weapon of

Mourners put up a Star of David for each of the eleven Jewish people who were killed in the shooting spree at the Tree of Life synagogue in Pittsburgh. Because the shooter targeted a Jewish congregation, the mass killings are considered hate crimes.

choice for many mass shooters. Other high-profile shootings in which killers used the weapon include a Christmas party in San Bernardino, California, in 2015 and a concert in Las Vegas in 2017.

Anti-Semitism, or hatred of Jews, fueled the synagogue crime. And the shooter's legal access to powerful weaponry raises the question, How much firepower is too much?

THE ARMS WE BEAR

When the founders wrote the Second Amendment, gun technology was in its infancy. Guns were slow-loading, heavy, and cumbersome. Their accuracy and range were poor. Mainly, craftsmanship and ease of maintenance made one gun superior to another.

The founders could not have envisioned modern gun technology such as automatic weapons, rocket-propelled grenades, and sawed-off shotguns. In the wording of the amendment, the founders did not distinguish among the firearms American could purchase and keep. In the young United States, weapons differed little in terms of destructive power. In the twenty-first century, many Americans argue that in this respect, the Second Amendment is obviously and badly outdated.

The leap forward in gun technology poses a difficult challenge for twenty-first-century scholars and lawmakers. They must decide: Does the Second Amendment guarantee the right to own all arms? Or does it give everyone the right to gun ownership while restricting the types of weapons Americans can legally own? Are a person's Second Amendment rights unfairly limited if allowed to own a handgun or a hunting rifle but not a fully automatic assault rifle? Where do we draw the line?

The US judicial system first grappled with this issue in 1939. Two men had been arrested for carrying an unregistered shotgun with a barrel of less than 18 inches (46 cm) from one state to another. This was a violation of the National Firearms Act of 1934. The men's attorneys argued that this law violated their clients' Second Amendment rights. The case, *United States v. Miller,* went all the way to the US Supreme Court.

The high court's justices determined that the National Firearms Act of 1934 did not violate the Second Amendment. Justice James McReynolds wrote, "In the absence of any evidence tending to show that possession or use of a 'shotgun having a barrel of less than eighteen inches [46 cm] in length' . . . has some reasonable relationship to the preservation or efficiency of a well regulated militia, we cannot say that the Second Amendment guarantees the right to keep and bear such an instrument. Certainly it is not [obvious to the court] that this weapon is any part of the ordinary military equipment or that its use could contribute to the common defense." The court said that the government does have the right to limit the types of firearms citizens can own.

United States v. Miller leaves room for interpretation, however. The ruling says that the government *can* dictate which weapons the Second Amendment protects. But people still argue about whether the government *should* do so. If the answer is yes, which arms are in and which are out? Modern weaponry is as varied as it is advanced.

ASSAULT WEAPONS

Most privately owned guns in the United States are used for self-defense, hunting, sport shooting, and collecting. Contrary to what some gun-rights advocates claim, US lawmakers have never shown real interest in creating or changing laws to make it overly difficult for law-abiding citizens to buy guns for these purposes. Some Americans view waiting periods and background checks as unfair hurdles to owning a gun. But most experts point out that these regulations don't stop responsible people from owning weapons. They just slow down the process. Lawmakers have shown interest, however, in banning weapons that go beyond gun owners' basic needs. Ultralong-range sniper rifles, automatic and semiautomatic weapons, high-caliber weapons, and armor-piercing ammunition are better suited for the military than for self-defense, hunting, or sport shooting. And consumers can purchase bump stocks to turn semiautomatic weapons into fully automatic weapons. Bump stocks allow the guns to shoot multiple rounds with a single pull of the trigger.

Should US law keep such powerful weapons away from ordinary Americans? Some people believe that it should. They think that such weaponry serves no purpose outside military settings. It can only lead to unnecessary harm. Others think that if the Second Amendment guarantees the right to bear arms, it guarantees the right to bear all arms. They believe

THE AK-47

The AK-47 automatic rifle is one of the most famous guns in history. It has been the model for countless other automatic and semiautomatic weapons, including the AR-15, which has been used in many mass shootings.

Russian military officer Mikhail Kalashnikov developed the AK-47 in the 1940s, perfecting it in 1947. AK-47 stands for Avtomat Kalashnikova 47 (Kalashnikov Automatic Rifle, 1947 model). Over time, the AK-47 proved to be a highly reliable and durable weapon. More than seven decades after its release, armies, citizens, and terrorist groups around the world still use the AK-47.

Bump stocks are easy to insert into a weapon such as this AK-47. They allow the gun to shoot multiple rounds with a single pull of the trigger.

Many countries, including the United States, prohibit private citizens from owning automatic weapons. Many assault weapons laws ban the AK-47 and its derivatives (spin-offs) by name. That creates a loophole. New versions of the gun, bearing different names, are generally not included in the bans. So gun manufacturers have altered AK-47 derivatives to make them into semiautomatic weapons. Semiautomatic versions of the AK-47 make up a large portion of the assault weapons whose legality is so hotly debated.

lawmakers should not choose which arms are legally available to Americans. If gun ownership is a check against tyranny, they argue, citizens need to be able to own military-grade weapons.

"We should ban possession of military-style semiautomatic assault weapons, we should buy back such weapons from all who choose to abide by the law, and we should criminally prosecute any who choose to defy it by keeping their weapons."

—US representative Eric Swalwell, California, 2018

The federal assault weapons ban of 1994 was one key limit to ownership of high-powered weaponry. Generally, it defined assault weapons as automatic weapons (which were already banned) or as semiautomatic weapons. A semiautomatic weapon automatically loads another round of ammunition, ready to fire, after each pull of the trigger. The ban included nineteen specific semiautomatic gun models by name. But the ban left many loopholes. It applied only to guns manufactured after the ban took effect. Gun manufacturers could make minor changes to their weapons to get around the ban. The consensus—on both sides of the gun-control debate—was that the ban had little effect on the flow of assault weapons into the hands of average gun owners.

The ban expired in 2004. The US Senate crushed a ten-year extension of the ban by a vote of 90–8. The issue of a new assault weapons ban has come up many times since 2004. In 2013 Democratic senator Dianne Feinstein introduced a new version of the ban—one that would not expire. However, the Senate voted it down by 60–40. Democrats introduced another version of the ban in 2018, though it has yet to come up for a vote.

Opponents of a new ban argue that since the first ban didn't work, Americans have no reason to think another one will.

BUMP STOCKS AND THE
LAS VEGAS SHOOTING

Country music pumped out of the speakers at the October 1, 2017, Route 91 Harvest music festival near the Mandalay Bay hotel in Las Vegas, Nevada. About twenty-two thousand music fans gathered for the outdoor music festival to listen to songs from their favorite country artists.

But starting at about 10:05 p.m., a different kind of noise brought the music to a swift halt. Bullets rained down on the festival from a window on the thirty-second floor of the hotel. Inside, a single gunman was opening fire on the helpless concertgoers. In about ten minutes, the sixty-four-year-old shooter fired eleven hundred rounds into the crowd, killing fifty-eight people and wounding many more. He used as many as twenty-four different guns to carry out the attack. Many of them were fitted with a bump stock, an aftermarket part that allows the weapons to be fired like automatic rifles. With a single pull of the trigger, the shooter could unleash an entire magazine full of bullets.

It was the deadliest mass shooting carried out by a single shooter in the history of the United States. It immediately threw bump stocks into the center of the gun-control debate. Until then bump stocks were largely unknown outside of the gun-collecting community. After the tragic shooting, gun-control supporters immediately demanded regulations on bump stocks. Even the NRA, which opposes almost any form of gun control, supports stronger regulations of bump stocks. In 2018 Trump proposed legislation that would effectively ban bump stocks. With support from both sides of the debate, the law appears likely to pass.

Concertgoers help the wounded during a mass shooting at a country music festival in Las Vegas in 2017.

Meanwhile, supporters of a new ban blame the NRA and other pro-gun groups for the ban's failure. They claim that the groups pressured politicians into voting against the original bill so that only a weak, ineffective law could pass. Without gun-lobby interference, supporters say, a stronger bill could get the job done.

"Millions and millions of law-abiding Americans use semiautomatic firearms with detachable magazines of varying capacities, and millions and millions of them every day don't do a thing wrong. You can't say that these guns bring out the worst in people. They're guns. They're neutral objects."
—Steve Sanetti, president and chief executive officer, National Shooting Sports Foundation, 2013

HANDGUNS

Handguns are another battleground in the gun-control debate. Unlike long-barreled rifles and shotguns, handguns aren't useful for hunters. Because a handgun has a short barrel, it doesn't have the long-range accuracy hunters need. Likewise, sport shooters rarely use handguns. Someone who draws a handgun, other than at a shooting range, is probably going to aim it at another person.

Some people see handguns as a dangerous threat because they are easy to conceal and easy to operate. A person doesn't need much gun knowledge or skill to wield a handgun effectively. Almost anybody, including a child, can pick up and use a handgun—unlike a rifle, which requires a certain amount of strength and competence. The vast majority of shooting accidents and crimes in the United States involve handguns. So some Americans want to ban handguns or at least control them more tightly.

PRINTABLE GUNS

Gun-control laws have always struggled to keep pace with technology. However, some experts believe that technology is outpacing policy in a terrifying new way. Americans may no longer need to go to a store or a gun show to purchase a gun. They may simply be able to download and print one right at home, using a 3D printer.

The idea behind 3D printing has been around since the 1980s. However, the technology didn't grow useful until the early twenty-first century. And it only started to become widely available—and affordable—to the public in the 2010s. Modern 3D printers, sold over the counter, can create everything from toys to car parts . . . to guns. In 2013, for example, visitors downloaded the free blueprint for one 3D gun, the Liberator .380, more than one hundred thousand times. The weapon, designed and released by gun enthusiast Cody Wilson, was the first of its kind to be widely available for download. New designs have surfaced online for semiautomatic weapons such as the AR-15.

It's still difficult for most people to print their own gun. As of 2018, 3D printers that can handle the job cost $5,000 or more. The guns usually are made from plastic material, and without high-grade plastic, the guns may not be durable enough to withstand the heat generated by a single shot. But as 3D printer technology grows and costs drop, it could be easy for anyone to simply go online, download plans for a gun, and print it. A person could do it all outside of any regulations, including background checks. And plastic guns are not detectable in most security scans. Since legislation has not yet caught up to the technology, the legal status of such guns remains unclear. It's a nightmare scenario for people who want to see fewer guns on the street.

Cody Wilson holds a 3D-printed gun he developed, the Liberator .380, in his factory in Texas.

Other people see the size and simplicity of handguns in a positive light. They argue that handguns are vital self-defense tools, especially for smaller or weaker gun owners who have difficulty handling larger guns. Handguns, they say, are equalizers. With a handgun, anyone can defend against an accomplished criminal. Gun-rights supporters say that balancing the playing field is the very reason the founders protected Americans' right to keep and bear arms.

CONTROLLING AMMUNITION

The gun-control debate isn't always about guns. Sometimes it's about ammunition. Most bullets go straight through a target. But specialty ammo behaves differently. Manufacturers produce several kinds of specialty ammunition, each designed to impact in different ways. They make armor-piercing ammunition from ultrahard metal such as tungsten, steel, brass, bronze, and iron. Incendiary ammo contains chemicals that ignite on impact. Fragmentation ammo shatters on impact, launching many deadly shards of metal. It includes ammo such as hollow-point bullets, which mushroom

"Let's face it—all guns can be used to kill people. But so can hammers, screw drivers and cars. That doesn't mean that they were designed for that purpose. There are more than 300 million firearms in the United States. There are about 9,000 murders and 500 accidents committed with those firearms in a given year. Roughly one gun out of 42,000 is used to kill someone. Add in suicides and the ratio becomes 1 in 12,500. If guns were actually designed to kill people, their designers are doing a lousy job."
—Dean Weingarten, gun-rights journalist, 2016

(expand) on impact, and flechette ammo, which is filled with projectiles that are released on impact. Exploding bullets contain chemicals that create small explosions on impact. Large-caliber ammunition refers to extra-large bullets and other large projectiles fired from guns. High-capacity magazines are ammo-feeding devices that hold large amounts of ammo.

Federal and state laws place some controls on the sale of ammunition. Most are similar to laws that limit gun sales. However, most Americans support more controls on specialty ammunition. Congress has passed laws that address this. For example, the Gun Control Act of 1968 bans certain types of armor-piercing ammunition. Those who support the ban argue that such ammo endangers police and other law enforcement officers who wear armor when facing off against criminals. The assault weapon ban of 1994 banned high-capacity magazines on the premise that no civilian needs more than a few shots for self-defense. Restrictions on other types of ammunition vary by state. In some states, such as New York and California, ammunition sales must be carefully tracked and reported. Yet states such as Missouri and Tennessee have virtually no state-level restrictions.

Opponents to restrictions on specialty ammunition say that it's not the government's place to decide how civilians defend themselves. They also point out that ammo restrictions don't stop criminals from using illegal ammunition. Instead, they argue that limiting the access of law-abiding citizens puts criminals at an advantage.

HEAVY ARTILLERY

Most of the US debate over the right to keep and bear arms focuses on guns. But what about other weapons? Does the Second Amendment cover heavy artillery such as rocket launchers, grenade launchers, high explosives, and missiles? These weapons serve no purpose in self-defense, hunting, or sport shooting. The US government keeps these military weapons away from common citizens. But some Americans say this is unconstitutional. Some Americans argue that the Second Amendment ensures that private citizens have whatever weaponry they need to overthrow an invading force or a tyrant threatening the home. Hunting rifles and handguns wouldn't do the job, they say. Neither would assault weapons. An invading army, for example, would have armored vehicles, heavy machine guns, and high explosives. Private citizens wouldn't stand a chance unless they were similarly armed.

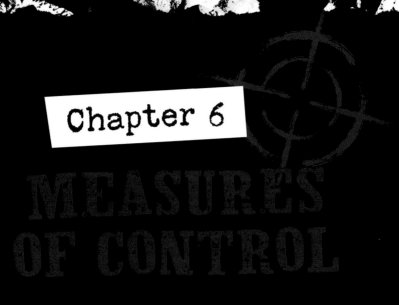

Chapter 6

MEASURES OF CONTROL

In 2012 Michael Joseph Henry went on a shopping spree. The Philadelphia, Pennsylvania, man went to several gun stores, where he purchased seven handguns and two rifles. Henry was not a convicted felon. He passed the state's background checks and bought the guns legally.

But Henry didn't buy the guns for himself. Soon after he bought them, he illegally sold them to Andrew Charles Thomas. As a convicted felon, Thomas couldn't buy firearms legally. Henry's purchase of the guns for him was a straw purchase. Henry sold the guns to support his drug habit. He knew that Thomas likely would use the guns against law enforcement. Soon after, law enforcement pursued Thomas after a hit-and-run crash. He used one of those guns to shoot and kill police officer Bradley Fox. Thomas then turned the gun on himself and killed himself.

Authorities traced the gun to its last legal owner. They arrested and charged Henry on a variety of counts. One year later, Henry was convicted and sentenced to a minimum of twenty years in prison. At his sentencing trial, Henry apologized

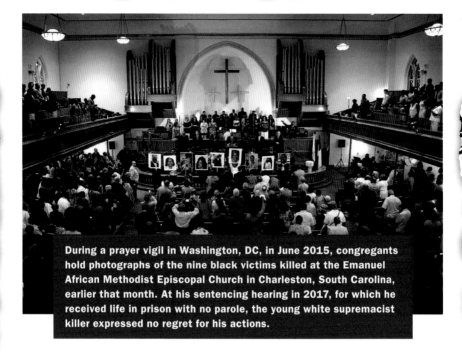

During a prayer vigil in Washington, DC, in June 2015, congregants hold photographs of the nine black victims killed at the Emanuel African Methodist Episcopal Church in Charleston, South Carolina, earlier that month. At his sentencing hearing in 2017, for which he received life in prison with no parole, the young white supremacist killer expressed no regret for his actions.

to the family of the slain officer. "I can't imagine the pain you go through," he said. "I have no one to blame but myself. I was not thinking about the consequences."

Henry's tragic decision had drastic consequences. He never pulled the trigger on the guns he bought, but his choice to ignore gun laws ended in death and heartbreak.

LICENSING AND REGISTRATION

Teenagers in every US state know that they need a license to drive a car. Motor vehicles are large, powerful, and potentially dangerous machines. To drive one legally, a person must first pass a test to demonstrate the ability to operate it safely. Yet while people need a license to operate a motor vehicle, no such federal requirement exists for firearms. No federal law requires gun licensing, registration, or permits.

These regulations are set in motion within individual states, and gun-licensing and registration laws vary by state. Some states require full licensing and registration of all firearms, while other states require only a permit to carry and conceal a weapon. Some states actually prohibit registration of any kind.

Some gun-control supporters believe that comprehensive federal guidelines for licensing and registration are desperately needed. They argue that gun use should follow the same standard as driving motor vehicles. They point out that guns are highly dangerous weapons and that misuse can endanger human lives. The federal government has a responsibility to make sure gun owners know how to handle their guns safely and responsibly. Just as a driver's test ensures basic competence among licensed drivers, so would gun licensing among gun owners. And registration of guns helps law enforcement organizations track guns used in crimes. Registration lists track gun owners and the guns they own, providing a valuable database in criminal investigations.

Gun-rights supporters strongly oppose federally mandated licensing and registration. They see both as dangerous steps toward revoking Second Amendment rights. They say that with required licensing and registration, a right guaranteed by the Constitution becomes a privilege granted by the government. The Second Amendment grants all Americans the right to keep and bear arms—not just the Americans the government views as responsible enough to do so or the Americans who are willing to register their firearms. Gun-rights supporters also argue that a tyrannical government could use licensing and registration lists to disarm a population. Such a government could use these lists to identify gun owners and seize their weapons, leaving the citizenry defenseless.

BALLISTIC IMAGING AND MICROSTAMPING

Matching a bullet to the gun that fired it is an important and a difficult job for forensic examiners in a criminal investigation. Traditionally, investigators have relied on ballistic imaging to connect a bullet to the gun that fired it. Every gun leaves a unique mark on the shell casings it fires—a sort of fingerprint that investigators can use to identify the gun used. However, this is time-consuming. And to make a match, the process requires that a database have a previous example of a bullet fired from the same gun.

Microstamping is one of the newest technologies that give law enforcement a quicker and more efficient way of tracing a gun. Firearm microstamping, also called ballistic imprinting and ballistic engraving, gives each gun a unique "fingerprint." A microstamped gun has a small laser-engraved design on its firing pin. This microstamp leaves a unique mark on the casing of fired ammunition. The gun and the casing each have the same stamp. So the mark tells police exactly which gun fired the bullet. Police can then check sales and registration records to get a lead on the case. Not all gun manufacturers build microstamping into their guns, however, and those who print 3D guns can easily bypass microstamping.

In 2013 California enacted a law requiring microstamping in semiautomatic weapons sold in that state. The law was challenged and then upheld in 2018. However, some gun companies refused to add the technology. Among them was Smith & Wesson. The company said, "Smith & Wesson does not and will not include microstamping in its firearms. The microstamping mandate and the company's unwillingness to adopt this so-called technology will result in a diminishing number of Smith & Wesson semiautomatic pistols available for purchase by California residents." The company disagreed with the law so strongly that it was willing to abandon one of the largest gun markets in the nation.

Federal laws do, however, address the licensing of firearms dealers. (This type of licensing applies only to people who sell physical guns. The distribution of plans for 3D guns is not covered.) The Gun Control Act of 1968 and the Firearm

Owners' Protection Act of 1986 require certain gun and ammunition sellers to obtain a Federal Firearms License. Licensed dealers must submit buyers' names for background checks. However, not everyone selling guns has to have a federal license. The requirement applies only to sellers who meet certain standards, such as those who sell firearms at retail or wholesale prices or who make their primary living dealing in firearms. Individual collectors who sell their firearms—a common practice at gun shows—do not have to obtain a license and do not have to do background checks. Some people want to close this loophole. Why should some dealers have to be licensed but not others? For gun-control advocates, the solution is to ensure that every firearms seller is licensed. Meanwhile, some gun-rights supporters suggest abandoning the flawed federal licensing system altogether, leaving everything in the hands of individual states.

BACKGROUND CHECKS

Background checks are another way to control the flow of guns in the United States. The Brady Handgun Violence Prevention Act of 1993 mandates such checks in all fifty states. At first, background checks took several days. Buyers had to wait five days between applying for a gun purchase and completing the purchase.

In November 1998, the FBI unveiled the National Instant Criminal Background Check System. Using this electronic system, federally licensed gun dealers can perform an instant background check on anyone trying to purchase a firearm. The dealer completes a document called a Firearms Transaction Record. It includes information about the buyer and the gun. The dealer submits this document to the NICS, which informs the dealer of the buyer's status within minutes. The dealer gets one of three responses:

1. Proceed. This response allows the dealer to complete the transaction according to applicable state laws.
2. Denied. This response means that the background check turned up information—usually a criminal record—that prevents the buyer from legally owning a firearm.
3. Delayed. This response means that the background check turned up information that might prevent the buyer from legally owning a firearm, but the information is incomplete and requires further investigation. Officials have three days to contact the dealer with an approval or a denial. If the dealer does not hear from officials within three days, the dealer can complete the sale.

Since the background-check system began, it has stopped more than 1.3 million gun sales to people who couldn't legally buy a gun. Supporters say this number shows that background checks slow the flow of guns to people who shouldn't have guns. Meanwhile, opponents of background checks argue that they are only partly effective. They don't prevent straw purchases, and they don't apply to transactions between individuals. Sometimes background checks get information wrong. A person who has the same name as a convicted felon, for example, may encounter difficulties. The information in the database is entered manually. If someone enters data incorrectly, a dangerous criminal may slip through the cracks or a dealer may wrongly deny a law-abiding citizen's gun purchase. Other critics argue that background checks are an invasion of privacy. Opponents believe that the

"Background checks, like all gun-control laws, focus on the law-abiding while mostly ignoring criminals. . . . The real objective is not reducing crime and violence, but rather to add impediments to legal gun ownership to discourage it and make it more costly, troublesome, and legally risky."

—Jeff Knox, director of the Firearms Coalition, 2015

background-check system is badly flawed and that its drawbacks outweigh its benefits.

WAITING PERIODS

Legislators have also turned to waiting periods to control the sales of firearms. Seventeen states and Washington, DC, have laws requiring waiting periods. These laws mandate that anyone purchasing a firearm wait a set amount of time before they can take possession of a gun they have purchased. Most waiting periods, passed at the state level, are only a few days. Waiting periods are designed to create a cooling-off period for anyone who wishes to buy a gun for the wrong reasons. A suicidal person may change their mind between buying a gun and taking it home. And a person intent on committing a violent crime may have time to rethink the decision.

According to a 2017 study led by Michael Luca of Harvard Business School, "Waiting period laws that delay the purchase of firearms by a few days reduce gun homicides by roughly 17 percent. Our results imply that the 17 states (including the District of Columbia) with waiting periods avoid roughly 750 gun homicides per year as a result of this policy. Expanding the waiting period policy to all other US states would prevent an additional 910 gun homicides per year without imposing any restrictions on who can own a gun."

Gun-rights supporters argue that waiting periods are an unnecessary inconvenience for law-abiding citizens. They also argue that waiting periods violate the Second Amendment because the government is removing a person's right to bear arms, even if only for a short time.

GUN SHOWS

Gun shows are big business in the United States, contributing more than $51 billion to the US economy. Gun manufacturers, dealers, and enthusiasts gather at gun shows to display, buy, sell, trade, and discuss firearms of all kinds. Manufacturers often use these events to show off new models and new features. Gun shows are a celebration of all things gun related and a place for gun enthusiasts to talk about and show off their collections. But gun shows are a source of controversy too. Many Americans worry about how guns are bought and sold there. Federal firearms licensees must always run background checks on buyers, even at gun shows. But only some of the vendors at gun shows are licensees. Shows also

Gun shows in some states allow unlicensed vendors to sell guns without having to do background checks on the people who purchase the weapons.

host many informal, unlicensed vendors. In many states, unlicensed vendors can legally buy and sell guns at shows without performing background checks at all.

Gun-control activists argue that this is an unacceptable loophole in gun law. Americans have invested a great deal of time and effort in crafting laws meant to keep guns out of the wrong hands. Many gun-control laws are useless if anyone can walk into a gun show and walk out with a gun. Allowing some vendors to ignore the background-check system invalidates the point of the system altogether, critics argue.

Gun enthusiasts counter that gun shows are an important part of gun culture in the United States. The shows offer gun owners a sense of community and serve as an educational tool. Small vendors are not required to have a federal license or seek background checks. Some people don't see gun shows as a significant source of guns used in crime. They don't think that the irresponsible actions of a few criminals should ruin the experience for all the law-abiding citizens who enjoy the shows.

Some states have passed laws to close the gun show loophole. But support for a bill at the federal level has been difficult to generate. Several bills were introduced in 2017 to address the loophole. Among them was the Gun Show Loophole Closing Act of 2017, proposed by US representative Carolyn Maloney of New York. Democrats supporting the bill hope that it will not fail, as have many earlier bills, including the Gun Show Loophole Closing Act of 2009 and the Gun Show Background Check Act of 2009. As of 2018, Maloney's bill still had not come to a vote.

CONCEALED CARRY

It's one thing to own a gun. The Second Amendment protects that right. But do Americans have the right to carry guns in public? And if so, do they have the right to conceal their weapons? All fifty states and the District of Columbia allow people to carry concealed guns. Permit requirements vary by state. They may include residency, age, fingerprinting, passing a background check, attending a gun-safety class, and paying a fee. The NRA is pushing for federal legislation that would require all states to recognize concealed carry permits from every other state, regardless of a state's permit laws.

Permits to conceal and carry a weapon in public fall into three categories:

1. Unrestricted (six states). Unrestricted states do not require permits to carry concealed guns.
2. Shall issue (thirty-five states). A shall-issue state issues concealed carry permits to all individuals who meet the permit's requirements. This category includes limited discretion and no-discretion groups. Limited discretion states allow for exceptions in certain cases. No-discretion states do not.
3. May issue (nine states). A may-issue state gives local authorities the power to decide which qualified applicants will receive permits. Applicants may have to provide some reason for needing to carry and conceal weapons.

What are the pros and cons of allowing private citizens to carry concealed weapons? Should the US government restrict concealed carry rights? How much? Some gun-control advocates think concealed carry laws need to be stricter. They argue that citizens carrying loaded guns in public are a danger to everyone. In 2018 twenty-nine-year-old Dane Gallion of Washington went to a movie. He was so concerned about the threat of a mass shooting that he brought his handgun with

"For too long, we have allowed the gun show loophole to undermine our best efforts to prevent crime and keep guns away from dangerous individuals. The Brady Bill has prevented the sale of more than 3 million guns to felons, domestic abusers, and other prohibited purchasers. The gun show loophole and other shortcomings erode this progress and safety check, allowing dangerous individuals to game the system and slip through the cracks."

—US representative Carolyn Maloney on the Gun Show Loophole Closing Act of 2017

him, loaded and tucked into the waistband of his pants. About fifteen minutes into the movie, the gun accidentally discharged. The bullet struck the woman sitting in front of Gallion. He rushed out of the theater, discarding his gun along the way. Soon he was arrested and charged with third-degree assault. The woman was hospitalized and survived. Cases like these lead many to believe that concealed guns do more harm than good and that concealed carry should be restricted on a federal level.

Meanwhile, many gun-rights supporters think concealed carry restrictions go too far. The threat of an armed citizen is a powerful crime deterrent, they say. Criminals are likely to carry weapons regardless of whether they have permits. So permit restrictions apply only to law-abiding citizens. Gun-rights supporters argue that restricting law-abiding citizens from carrying firearms leaves everyone less safe. When criminals know that citizens are unlikely to be carrying weapons, they have less fear of carrying out their crimes.

GUN-FREE ZONES

Even when a person has legal permission to carry a gun, that person can't do so everywhere. In 1990 the US Congress passed the Gun-Free School Zones Act. This federal law declared schools and the areas around them to be gun-free zones. In 1994 the Fifth Circuit court struck down the law as unconstitutional in *United States v. Lopez.* (The US Supreme Court affirmed the circuit court's decision a year later.) Congress quickly replaced the law with the Gun-Free Schools Act of 1994. This law is a revised version of the 1990 law. It places strict limitations on where citizens can carry firearms. It forbids any firearms on school grounds (kindergarten through twelfth grade) or in public areas (streets, sidewalks, and so on) within 1,000 feet (305 m) of a school. States can grant exemptions to individual permit holders.

State and federal laws allow for many other gun-free zones. These include post offices, hospitals, shopping malls, churches, polling places, and more. Some states allow individual businesses to prohibit weapons on their property.

Supporters of gun-free zones argue that they protect innocents, especially children. Laws that keep guns away from schools and other vulnerable areas can reduce children's risk of becoming the victims of gun violence.

Opponents argue the opposite. They say that criminals ignore the law, and laws designating gun-free zones are no exception. If a criminal went on a shooting rampage in a gun-free zone, no one would

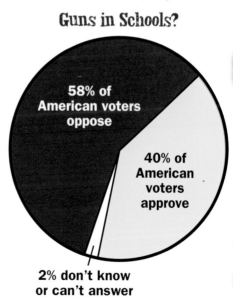

Guns in Schools?

58% of American voters oppose

40% of American voters approve

2% don't know or can't answer

Source: Quinnipiac University Poll, 2018

have the firepower to stop that person. Furthermore, opponents argue that gun-free zones are unconstitutional because they strip people of their Second Amendment rights.

According to a 2016 study by the Crime Prevention Research Center, 98.4 percent of mass shootings occur in gun-free zones—mainly schools. (This data excludes shootings related to drug and gang crime.) This has led the NRA and its supporters—including Trump—to propose eliminating all gun-free zone laws.

GUN BUYBACKS

In recent decades, city leaders across the United States have become worried about the number of guns on the streets, especially among youth. Many cities, through their police departments, have started programs to remove some of these guns from circulation. These programs, often called gun buybacks, offer cash (from $25 to $250), gift cards, or other incentives in exchange for each gun. In most programs, anyone can exchange a gun with no questions asked. Whether buyback programs work is debatable. Supporters point to programs that bring in thousands of guns. One program in Washington, DC, took more than four thousand guns off the street. Someone even turned in two hand grenades. Supporters of gun buybacks say that every gun taken off the street is one gun that cannot be used in an illegal or accidental shooting. By reducing the number of guns in an area, gun buybacks can reduce gun violence.

But do buybacks really reduce gun violence? The US Department of Justice says that guns turned in to buyback programs are least likely to have been used for crime. Criminals aren't the ones turning in their guns. That's irrelevant, according to some buyback supporters. They argue

that any gun off the
streets is a gun that
can't fall into the wrong
hands. According to
Santa Fe, New Mexico,
police chief Raymond
Rael, "Even one tragedy
prevented; even one
suicide, or one child
who accesses an
unsecured weapon and
has an accidental shooting; I think
the program pays for itself, and it's
well worth it."

Los Angeles is one of many communities in the United States that periodically initiates gun buybacks. The programs recover only a small percentage of guns, but supporters believe the programs are worthwhile.

Some buyback skeptics point
out that even taking thousands
of guns off the streets makes little difference. "[Buyback
programs] make for good photo images," said Michael Scott,
director of the Center for Problem-Oriented Policing, based
at the University of Wisconsin Law School. "But gun buyback
programs recover such a small percentage of guns that it's not
likely to make much impact."

Supporters counter that gun buyback programs don't cost
much. They're one part of a larger effort, and every piece matters.

RED FLAG LAWS

One of the more recent developments in gun control is red
flag laws, also called gun violence restraining orders, or
extreme risk protection order laws. These laws, passed at
the state level, allow family members or law enforcement to
seek temporary court orders to restrict people who might be a
danger to themselves or others from having firearms.

The laws vary by state. But the process is the same. A person—usually a family member—can go before a judge to provide evidence that an individual is showing alarming behavior, or red flags, that pose a threat. If the judge agrees, a temporary order is issued to have law enforcement seize any firearms the troubled individual might possess. Before the 2018 Parkland, Florida, shootings, five states had red flag laws. The Parkland shooter had a long history of red flag behavior, including emotional problems and gun violence interactions with authorities. After the tragedy at the high school, at least twenty-two states either passed or introduced legislation for red flag laws.

For many, red flag laws seem like an easy and obvious solution to help stem both suicide and mass shootings. Even the NRA has given the laws a measure of support. "We need to stop dangerous people before they act," said Chris Cox, executive director for the NRA's Institute for Legislative Action.

But many gun-rights advocates see them as dangerous. They feel that the laws allow the government to take away a person's Second Amendment rights, even when they have done nothing wrong. This form of preventive justice—prior restraint—takes away something dangerous before a crime or harmful event can occur. Those who oppose such laws fear that red flag laws set a dangerous precedent and threaten the Second Amendment rights of all Americans. "They think you might do something bad, so they're going to take away your civil rights," said Dudley Brown, president of the National Association for Gun Rights.

ARMING TEACHERS

In recent years, the idea of arming teachers in schools has been debated. Donald Trump supported the idea after the

2018 Parkland, Florida, shooting. The argument in favor of arming teachers is simple. If someone enters a school with the intent to kill, law enforcement won't be able to respond in time to stop them. The best chance to end a shooting spree is for a rapid response from within the school. Teachers trained to use deadly force in such a situation would be able to reduce the harm done by a shooter.

"Some school districts, they promote it," said Greg Abbott, governor of Texas. "Because they will have signs out front—a warning sign: 'Be aware, there are armed personnel on campus'—warning anybody coming on there that they—if they attempt to cause any harm, they're going to be in trouble."

Others say that arming teachers presents more problems than it solves. Bringing weapons into the school increases the likelihood of accidents or misuse. And many argue that teachers are not suited to using deadly force against students. Jesse Wasmer was a guidance counselor at Perry Hall High School, in Baltimore, Maryland, when a student opened fire there in 2012. Wasmer tackled the shooter, probably saving many lives. "Never have I thought, 'I wish I'd had a gun,'" Wasmer said. "I think as educators we're trained to nurture kids and foster kids, and our first instinct is to not shoot or harm them. What we need is more caring adults in these kids' lives, not more guns."

AN UNCERTAIN FUTURE

A century ago, almost no debate over gun control existed in the United States. Americans simply didn't worry much about gun rights or gun violence. But since then, concern over the issue has grown. Is gun ownership a danger to Americans, or does it keep the nation safe? What role should the government play in determining who can own firearms and which firearms they can own?

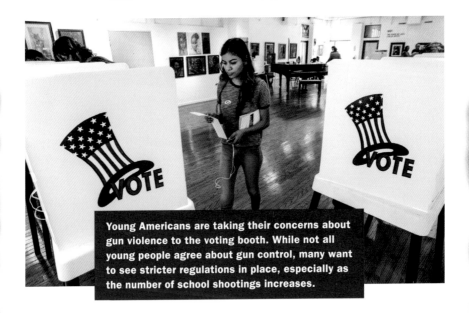

Young Americans are taking their concerns about gun violence to the voting booth. While not all young people agree about gun control, many want to see stricter regulations in place, especially as the number of school shootings increases.

With each passing decade, the debate has grown more hostile and the arguments more extreme. Legislation has grown increasingly abundant—and increasingly complicated. In the 1960s, Americans disagreed over strategies to reduce gun violence while protecting gun rights. But they also worked together toward compromise. Since then the two sides of the issue have drifted further and further apart. In the twenty-first century, gun-control and gun-rights advocates can't find common ground to build compromise. Each side has dug in its heels and refuses to budge. So the issue has become a political football—a matter that's debated but never resolved.

Most Americans fall somewhere between the two extremes. Most Americans treasure the liberties guaranteed by the Bill of Rights. Freedom of speech, freedom of religion, and the freedom to keep and bear arms are key elements of the greatness of the nation, they say. But polls reveal that most Americans believe some level of gun control is necessary. News programs and newspapers constantly deliver stories

THE SUPREME COURT AND THE FUTURE OF FEDERAL GUN LAW

Often, when Americans think about federal gun laws, they look to the White House and Congress. The president and members of both houses of Congress are key in forming and passing laws to strengthen or relax measures of gun control. And the US Supreme Court has the final say on which are constitutional.

In June 2018, Associate Justice Anthony Kennedy made a surprising announcement. He was retiring from the Supreme Court sooner than anticipated. Up until then, the court's nine justices included four conservatives, who tended to oppose gun control, and four liberals, who tended to support it. Kennedy was an important swing vote, someone who did not make decisions in a consistently conservative or liberal manner. With Kennedy's retirement, Trump nominated a conservative judge, Brett Kavanaugh, to the court. After controversial and heated hearings, the Senate voted to confirm Kavanaugh and swore him in on October 6, 2018. With the confirmation, the conservative-liberal balance tips conservative. Kavanaugh has traditionally ruled against gun-control laws, viewing the issue as a strictly constitutional manner while ignoring arguments of public safety. Because of his views, many supporters of gun control are alarmed. "I think there's a developing expectation that right-wing [conservative] judges invalidate any and all restrictions on the Second Amendment," said Senator Christopher S. Murphy of Connecticut. "I worry [Kavanaugh] will pull the court to a place where no state or municipality can exercise any oversight on gun laws."

about gun violence in the United States. Americans want their government to help ensure their safety. They differ on the best way for the government to do so.

The waves of protest, mainly by young people, following the Parkland, Florida, shooting in 2018 marks a new chapter in the debate. Young people, not willing to wait for their elders to solve the problem, have sought solutions to gun violence. As they reach the legal voting age of eighteen, they will use the ballot to make their voices heard.

TIMELINE

1100s   Debate rages in Europe over a deadly new weapon, the crossbow.

1300s   People develop modern firearms such as cannons and guns in both Europe and China.

1400s   Guns become common but remain clumsy.

1500s   Gun design starts advancing rapidly. European settlers begin moving to North America, establishing a culture of guns there.

1594   Queen Elizabeth I of England bans the wheel-lock pistol.

1775   The American Revolution begins.

1776   The thirteen colonies declare independence from Great Britain and form the United States of America.

1783   The American Revolution ends.

1787   The young United States adopts its Constitution.

1791   The United States ratifies the Bill of Rights. This document includes the Second Amendment, which grants Americans the right to keep and bear arms.

1871   William Church and George Wingate form the National Rifle Association.

1873   An election dispute erupts in Louisiana, leading to the US Supreme Court case *United States v. Cruikshank,* which determines that the Second Amendment applies only to the federal government, not to individuals or groups.

1927   To address the growing problem of organized crime, Congress passes the Mailing of Firearms Act, which outlaws the shipping of concealable handguns by US mail.

1934   Congress passes the National Firearms Act, which taxes the sales of short-barreled rifles and shotguns, automatic weapons, silencers, and explosive devices and requires registration for these weapons. The law does not include handguns.

1938   Congress passes the Federal Firearms Act, which bans the sale of firearms to convicted felons and fugitives and bars unlicensed dealers from selling guns across state lines.

1939   In *United States v. Miller,* the US Supreme Court rules that the government has the right to limit the types of firearms citizens may own.

1947   Mikhail Kalashnikov perfects the AK-47.

1963 Lee Harvey Oswald assassinates President John F. Kennedy using a cheap imported gun ordered through the NRA magazine the *American Rifleman.* The assassination reignites the gun-control debate.

1968 In response to a series of assassinations and violet riots, Congress passes the Gun Control Act, the nation's first comprehensive gun-control legislation. This law establishes the Bureau of Alcohol, Tobacco and Firearms.

1981 An assassination attempt on President Ronald Reagan seriously injures press secretary James Brady. He and his wife form the Brady Campaign to Prevent Gun Violence.

1986 Congress passes the Firearm Owners' Protection Act, scaling back the Gun Control Act of 1968.

1990 Congress passes the Gun-Free School Zones Act.

1993 Congress passes the Brady Handgun Violence Prevention Act, mandating background checks for gun purchasers.

1994 Congress passes the Violent Crime Control and Law Enforcement Act, which includes the federal assault weapons ban.

The US Fifth Circuit Court of Appeals strikes down the Gun-Free School Zones Act. Congress then revises the law and passes a new Gun-Free Schools Act.

1998 The FBI unveils the National Instant Criminal Background Check System, which allows gun dealers to perform instant background checks.

1999 Two students bring four guns and many homemade explosives to Columbine High School in Colorado, where they carry out a massacre that kills thirteen innocent people. This incident sparks a wave of gun-control debate.

2004 The federal assault weapons ban expires, and Congress declines to renew it.

2005 Congress passes the Protection of Lawful Commerce in Arms Act, shielding gun manufacturers and dealers from certain civil lawsuits related to gun violence.

2008 In *District of Columbia v. Heller,* the US Supreme Court rules that the Second Amendment guarantees individual gun rights.

2011 Jared Lee Loughner opens fire at a supermarket in Casas Adobes, Arizona. He kills six people and wounds thirteen others, including US representative Gabrielle Giffords. She and her husband later found the gun-control organization Americans for Responsible

Solutions, which merges in 2016 with the Law Center to Prevent Gun Violence to become the Giffords Law Center to Prevent Gun Violence.

2012 A gunman kills twenty-six people at Sandy Hook Elementary School in Newton, Connecticut.

2013 The blueprints for a 3D-printed gun, the Liberator .380, are downloaded more than one hundred thousand times.

2015 Fourteen people are gunned down in a mass shooting at a Christmas party at the Inland Regional Center in San Bernardino, California.

A twenty-one-year-old white supremacist kills nine black people during a prayer service at a Charleston, South Carolina, church. The shooter is sentenced to death for the hate crime.

2016 A shooter with ties to terrorist organizations kills forty-nine people inside a gay nightclub in Orlando, Florida. It is the bloodiest terrorist attack on US soil since the terror attacks of September 11, 2001.

2017 A single shooter kills fifty-eight people at a music concert from the window of a Las Vegas hotel. The shooter used a bump stock to turn his guns into automatic weapons. State and federal legislators introduce bills to ban bump stocks.

2018 A shooter at the Marjory Stoneman Douglas high school in Parkland, Florida, kills seventeen people. Survivors of the shooting and their allies launch the March for Our Lives movement with national protest marches on March 24, 2018. The organization also mobilizes young people to register to vote as part of the mission to demand more restrictive reforms to US gun laws.

A shooter enters a Pittsburgh, Pennsylvania, synagogue and opens fire. He guns down eleven people in one of the bloodiest hate crimes in recent US history.

2019 California enacts a law requiring background checks on all ammunition purchases.

GLOSSARY

assault weapons: automatic or semiautomatic weapons designed for military-type attacks

automatic weapon: a weapon that fires multiple rounds of ammunition with a single trigger pull

bump stock: an aftermarket part that converts a gun into an automatic weapon

cache: hidden supply

caliber: the diameter of a gun barrel or ammunition

castle law: a law that gives people the right to use lethal force to defend themselves from intruders in their homes

crossbow: a mechanized bow that fires short, heavy, pointed projectiles called bolts

felony: a serious crime, such as murder, sexual assault, or aggravated assault, which is often penalized with jail or prison time

handgun: a small handheld gun, such as a pistol

lobbying: trying to influence public officials to support a particular point of view or legislation

magazine: a clip that contains ammunition and feeds it into a weapon

microstamping: laser engraving a design on a gun's firing pin. This design leaves a unique mark on the casing of fired ammunition. Microstamping is also called ballistic imprinting, or ballistic engraving.

militia: a small, local, loosely organized military group

misdemeanor: a lesser crime than a felony. Misdemeanors include crimes such as petty theft, simple assault, disorderly conduct, and trespassing, and are often penalized with monetary fines rather than jail or prison time

National Rifle Association: an American nonprofit organization that advocates for gun rights. The NRA wields a great deal of political power and has tremendous influence over US gun laws.

red flag law: a law that allows a family member or law enforcement to petition a judge to have a person's firearms taken away temporarily, if they can demonstrate that the person is a danger to themselves or to others

rifle: a long gun with spiraling grooves engraved inside its barrel

semiautomatic weapon: a weapon that automatically and quickly makes new ammunition ready to fire after each pull of the trigger

shotgun: a long gun whose barrel is smooth inside

stand-your-ground laws: laws that permit individuals to use guns in self-defense when threatened

straw purchase: a transaction in which one person buys a firearm for another person

3D gun: a weapon, made from plastic, that is fabricated on a 3D printer and can easily skirt gun laws, such as background checks

tommy gun: a lightweight machine gun

SOURCE NOTES

5   Morgan Winsor and Jennifer Eccleston, "March for Our Lives Takes Place around the World, from London to Berlin to Sydney," *ABC News*, March 24, 2018, https://abcnews.go.com/International /march-lives-takes-place-world-london-berlin/story?id=53982310.

6   "Students Protest Gun Violence in D.C. March for Our Lives," *Washington Post*, March 24, 2018, https://www.washingtonpost .com/lifestyle/kidspost/students-protest-gun-violence-in-dc -march/2018/03/24/39995b0c-2fcf-11e8-8688-e053ba58f1e4_ story.html?utm_term=.0a651cd2b5b4.

6   "Students Protest."

6   "March for Our Lives Highlights: Students Protesting Guns Say 'Enough Is Enough,'" *New York Times*, March 24, 2018, https:// www.nytimes.com/2018/03/24/us/march-for-our-lives.html.

8   Joint Committee on Printing, "The Constitution of the United States with Index and the Declaration of Independence," Government Printing Office, July 25, 2007, http://frwebgate.access.gpo.gov /cgi-bin/getdoc.cgi?dbname=110_cong_documents&docid=f :hd051.110.pdf.

9   Glen Martin, "So, about That 'Well-Regulated Militia' Part of the Constitution," Cal Alumni Association, August 28, 2017, https:// alumni.berkeley.edu/california-magazine/just-in/2017-08-28/so -about-well-regulated-militia-part-constitution.

10   Michael A. Bellesiles, *Arming America: The Origins of a National Gun Culture* (New York: Alfred A. Knopf, 2000), 18.

15   Bellesiles, 76.

17   Bellesiles, 210.

17   Thomas Jefferson, "Thomas Jefferson to William Smith: November 13, 1787," Library of Congress, July 22, 2010, http://www.loc.gov /exhibits/jefferson/105.html.

26   Supreme Court of the United States, "Syllabus: District of Columbia et al. v. Heller," Cornell University Law School Legal Information Institute: Supreme Court Collection, June 26, 2008, http://www.law.cornell.edu/supct/html/07-290.ZS.html.

30   Victor Luckerson, "Read Barack Obama's Speech on New Gun Control Measures," *Time,* January 5, 2016, http://time .com/4168056/obama-gun-control-speech-transcript/.

30   Anne Gearan, Mike DeBonis, and Seung Min Kim, "Trump Surprises Lawmakers in Backing Some Tougher Gun Controls," *Washington Post*, February 28, 2018, https://www.washingtonpost.com /powerpost/democrats-rally-around-universal-background-checks -ahead-of-white-house-meeting/2018/02/28/13c4a5d2-1ca4 -11e8-9de1-147dd2df3829_story.html?utm_term=.ec98f2f55d0f.

30, 32   Jeff Mason and Daniel Trotta, "Trump Back in Step with NRA after Doubts over Parkland Shooting," Reuters, May 4, 2018, https:// www.reuters.com/article/us-usa-guns-trump/months-after-parkland -shooting-trump-to-embrace-nra-in-rally-like-speech-idUSKBN1 I50ZR.

36   Caleb Downs, "Sutherland Springs Hero Says He's 'Proof' Mainstream Media, Anti-Gun Activists Are Wrong," MySanAntonio .com, April 30, 2018, https://www.mysanantonio.com/news/local /article/Sutherland-Springs-hero-says-he-s-proof-12875242.php.

37   Robert Preidt, "How U.S. Gun Deaths Compare to Other Countries," *CBS News*, February 3, 2013, https://www.cbsnews.com/news /how-u-s-gun-deaths-compare-to-other-countries/.

39   Lois Beckett, "Trump Echoes Mexican President, Says Lax US Gun Laws Help Arm Drug Cartels," *Guardian* (US ed.), September 1, 2016, https://www.theguardian.com/us-news/2016/sep/01 /donald-trump-mexico-visit-guns-drug-cartels-nra.

45   Karin Kiewra, "Guns and Suicide: A Fatal Link," *Harvard Public Health Review*, Spring 2008, https://www.hsph.harvard.edu/news /magazine/guns-and-suicide/.

47   "Self-Defense Gun Use Is Rare, Study Finds," Violence Policy Center, June 17, 2015, http://vpc.org/press/self-defense-gun-use -is-rare-study-finds/.

47   Samantha Raphelson. "How Often Do People Use Guns In Self- Defense?," NPR, April 13, 2018, https://www.npr.org/2018 /04/13/602143823/how-often-do-people-use-guns-in-self -defense.

55   Jason Ryan, "247 on U.S. Terror Watch List Bought Guns in 2010," *ABC News*, April 28, 2011, https://abcnews.go.com/Blotter/247-us -terror-watchlist-bought-guns-2010/story?id=13480320.

55   Dana Milbank, "Terrorists Who Want to Buy Guns Have Friends on Capitol Hill," *Washington Post*, May 6, 2010, http:// www.washingtonpost.com/wp-dyn/content/article/2010 /05/05/AR2010050505211.html.

55   Milbank.

55 Milbank.

56 Jordain Carney, "Senators Introduce Bill to Block Terrorists from Buying Guns," *Hill*, February 27, 2018, http://thehill.com /homenews/senate/375824-senators-introduce-bill-to-block -terrorists-from-buying-guns.

57–58 Antonin Scalia, "Opinion of the Court: District of Columbia v. Heller," Cornell University Law School Legal Information Institute: Supreme Court Collection, June 26, 2008, http://www.law.cornell .edu/supct/html/07-290.ZO.html.

58–59 John P. Stevens, "Stevens, J., Dissenting: SUPREME COURT OF THE UNITED STATES DISTRICT OF COLUMBIA, et al., PETITIONERS v. DICK ANTHONY HELLER," Cornell University Law School, June 26, 2008, https://www.law.cornell.edu/supct/html/07-290.ZD.html

60 Ryan Cleckner, "Why More Gun Laws Won't Prevent Violence," Rocket FFL, November 15, 2017, https://rocketffl.com/why-more -gun-laws-wont-prevent-violence/.

62 Brett Samuels, "Trump: 'Take the Guns First, Go through Due Process Second,'" *Hill*, February 28, 2018, https://thehill.com /homenews/administration/376097-trump-take-the-guns-first-go -through-due-process-second.

62 Jonel Aleccia and Melissa Bailey, "'I Can't Imagine Living without Guns,' for Some, Dementia Is Forcing That Choice," *Idaho Statesman,* July 24, 2018, https://www.idahostatesman.com /living/health-fitness/article213868924.html.

68–69 James McReynolds, "Opinion of the Court: United States v. Miller*,"* Cornell University Law School Legal Information Institute: Supreme Court Collection, May 15, 1939, accessed December 3, 2010, http://www.law.cornell.edu/supct/html/historics/USSC_ CR_0307_0174_ZO.html.

71 Eric Swalwell, "Ban Assault Weapons, Buy Them Back, Go after Resisters: Ex-Prosecutor in Congress," *USA Today,* May 3, 2018, https://www.usatoday.com/story/opinion/2018/05/03/ban -assault-weapons-buy-them-back-prosecute-offenders-column /570590002/.

73 Matthew Kauffman, "A Deeper Divide: The Gun Control Debate after Newtown," *Hartford Courant,* February 19, 2013, https://www .courant.com/news/connecticut/newtown-sandy-hook-school -shooting/hc-gunstory-mainbar-20130219-story.html.

75 Dean Weingarten, "No Matter What You Hear, Guns Aren't Designed to Kill People," *The Truth about Guns* (blog), May 5, 2016, http://www.thetruthaboutguns.com/2016/05/dean-weingarten /guns-not-designed-kill-people/.

79   Carl Hessler Jr., "Gun Seller in Killing of Plymouth Officer Fox Sentenced to 20–66 Years," Mainline Media News, August 16, 2013, http://www.mainlinemedianews.com/news/region /gun-seller-in-killing-of-plymouth-officer-fox-sentenced-to /article_066fa62a-c03f-518c-a41b-adbbf6638a0b.html.

81   Perry Chiaramonte, "Gun Flight: Smith & Wesson, Ruger Quit California over Stamping Requirement," *Fox News*, last modified January 12, 2017, https://www.foxnews.com/us/gun-flight-smith -wesson-ruger-quit-california-over-stamping-requirement.

84   Michael Luca, Deepak Malhotra, and Christopher Poliquin, "Handgun Waiting Periods Reduce Gun Deaths," *Proceedings of the National Academy of Science,* available online at National Center for Biotechnology Information, October 16, 2017, https://www.ncbi .nlm.nih.gov/pmc/articles/PMC5699026/.

84   Jeff Knox, "Why Background Checks Don't Work," *WND*, March 5, 2015, https://www.wnd.com/2015/03/why-background-checks -dont-work/.

88   "Maloney Introduces Legislation to Close Gun Show Loophole," news release, Maloney.house.gov, March 17, 2017, https:// maloney.house.gov/media-center/press-releases/maloney -introduces-legislation-to-close-gun-show-loophole.

91   "Gun Buyback Programs Tend to Attract Low-Risk Groups," *NPR,* January 12, 2013, https://www.npr.org/2013/01/12/169209919 /gun-buyback-programs-tend-to-attract-low-risk-groups.

91   Dan Horn, "Gun Buybacks Popular but Ineffective, Experts Say," *USA Today,* January 13, 2013, https://www.usatoday.com /story/news/nation/2013/01/12/gun-buybacks-popular-but -ineffective/1829165/.

92   Michael Livingston, "More States Approving 'Red Flag' Laws to Keep Guns Away from People Perceived as Threats," *Los Angeles Times,* May 14, 2018, https://www.latimes.com/nation/la-na-red -flag-laws-20180514-story.html.

92   Livingston.

93   Erica L. Green and Manny Fernandez, "Trump Wants to Arm Teachers. These Schools Already Do," *New York Times,* March 1, 2018, https://www.nytimes.com/2018/03/01/us/armed-teachers -guns-schools.html.

93   Green and Fernandez.

95   Todd Ruger, "With Kavanaugh, Court Could Take Aim at Gun Control Laws," *Roll Call,* July 26, 2018, https://www.rollcall.com/news /politics/with-new-justice-court-could-take-aim-at-gun-control-laws.

SELECTED BIBLIOGRAPHY

Amar, Akhil Reed, and Les Adams. *The Bill of Rights Primer: A Citizen's Guidebook to the American Bill of Rights.* New York: Skyhorse, 2013.

"Assault Weapons." Giffords Law Center to Prevent Gun Violence. Accessed November 1, 2018. https://lawcenter.giffords.org/gun-laws/policy -areas/hardware-ammunition/assault-weapons/.

Berkin, Carol. *The Bill of Rights: The Fight to Secure America's Liberties.* New York: Simon & Schuster, 2015.

Carter, Gregg Lee. *Gun Control in the United States: A Reference Handbook.* 2nd ed. Santa Barbara, CA: ABC-CLIO, 2017.

Lott, John R. *More Guns Less Crime: Understanding Crime and Gun Control Laws.* Chicago: University of Chicago Press, 2010.

"Red Flag Laws and Firearm Suicide Prevention." Everytown. Accessed December 15, 2018. https://everytownresearch.org/red-flag-laws -firearm-suicide-prevention.

Spitzer, Robert J. *The Politics of Gun Control.* Boulder, CO: Paradigm, 2015.

Winkler, Adam. *Gunfight: The Battle over the Right to Bear Arms in America.* New York: W. W. Norton, 2013.

FURTHER INFORMATION

Books

Allen, John. *Thinking Critically: Gun Control.* San Diego: ReferencePoint, 2017.
The author challenges readers to think critically about the pros and cons of various gun-control issues.

Cook, Philip J., and Kristin A. Goss. *The Gun Debate: What Everyone Needs to Know.* Oxford: Oxford University Press, 2014. The authors provide a neutral viewpoint on the origins and history of the gun-control debate.

Falkowski, Melissa, and Eric Garner, eds. *We Say #NeverAgain: Reporting by the Parkland Student Journalists.* New York: Crown Books for Young Readers, 2018. This selection of writing by student reporters for the

Marjory Stoneman Douglas High School newspaper and TV station offers a window into their experience of the deadly shooting at their Florida high school and of the fight for gun control. Falkowski is the school's journalism teacher, and Garner is the broadcasting teacher there.

Goldsmith, Connie. *Understanding Suicide: A National Epidemic.* Minneapolis: Twenty-First Century Books, 2017.
Learn more about suicide and the reasons people turn to it. Learn the signs of suicide and how to address depression in this deeply researched book for YA readers, written by a nurse and medical journalist.

Hand, Carol. *Gun Control and the Second Amendment.* Minneapolis: Essential Library, 2017.
Read more about the Second Amendment and how it applies to the debate over gun control.

Hillstrom, Laurie Collier. *The Constitution and the Bill of Rights.* Detroit: Omnigraphics, 2017.
Learn more about the US Constitution and the Bill of Rights and how the documents are the law of the land.

Hogg, David, and Lauren Hogg. *#NeverAgain: A New Generation Draws the Line.* New York: Random House, 2018.
A sister and brother, both survivors of the Parkland, Florida, high school shooting, offer an in-depth look at the making of the #NeverAgain movement in this best-selling book.

The March for Our Lives founders. *Glimmer of Hope: How Tragedy Sparked a Movement.* New York: Razorbill, 2018.
This collaborative collection of essays by friends and family of Parkland victims discusses the March for Our Lives movement and the launch demonstration on March 24, 2018. They talk about how they turned their emotions into action, and the book also lays out the movement's goals. The authors decided not to take the proceeds from the book for themselves but to donate them to the March for Our Lives Action Fund.

Otfinoski, Steven. *Gun Control.* New York: Children's Press, 2014.
The author delves into many aspects of the gun-control debate, examining the pros and cons of gun control.

Streissguth, Tom. *District of Columbia v. Heller: The Right to Bear Arms Case.* Berkeley Heights, NJ: Enslow, 2010.
Discover the details of the landmark US Supreme Court case that found the right to bear arms is an individual right of all Americans.

Wolfe, James. *Understanding the Bill of Rights.* New York: Enslow, 2016.
The Bill of Rights sets out basic freedoms for all Americans. But it's not always clear just what the founders intended with some of these rights. Explore different ways of interpreting their words.

Films and Documentaries

Bowling for Columbine. DVD. Los Angeles: MGM, 2003.
In this Academy Award–winning documentary, activist filmmaker Michael Moore explores the reasons behind the high rate of gun violence in the United States.

Breslin, Kevin, dir. *Living for 32.* Breslin Films, 2011.
This short film tells the story of Colin Goddard, a survivor of a 2004 mass shooting that occurred on the campus of Virginia Polytechnic Institute and State University in Blacksburg, Virginia.

Richie, John, dir. *91%: A Film about Guns in America.* New York: Cinema Guild, 2016.
This film shares accounts of people impacted by gun violence and offers hope for common ground in the debate over guns in the United States.

Websites

American Firearms Institute
http://www.americanfirearms.org
The American Firearms Institute is a pro-gun organization that fights for gun rights in the United States. The website includes fact sheets, statistics, and information on federal and state gun laws.

Bill of Rights
http://www.archives.gov/exhibits/charters/bill_of_rights.html
Read the entire Bill of Rights, and see a photograph of the original document. The site also offers more information on other constitutional amendments.

Brady Campaign to Prevent Violence
http://www.bradycampaign.org/
The Brady Campaign provides visitors with the latest news in gun control, as well as ways to take action, contact politicians, and make their voices heard.

Bureau of Alcohol, Tobacco, Firearms and Explosives (ATF)
http://www.atf.gov
The ATF, a federal government agency, is responsible for protecting the United States against the illegal use and trafficking of firearms, the illegal use and storage of explosives, acts of arson and bombings, acts of terrorism, and the illegal diversion of alcohol and tobacco products. The ATF site provides details on gun laws, as well as a portal for submitting tips to law enforcement.

Coalition to Stop Gun Violence
http://www.csgv.org
The Coalition to Stop Gun Violence works to reduce gun violence in the United States through education, research, and political advocacy. Visitors can read more about a wide range of gun violence topics, including battling domestic abuse and preventing suicide.

Giffords Law Center to Prevent Gun Violence
https://lawcenter.giffords.org/
This comprehensive site provides in-depth statistics and infographics on gun violence, as well as detailed discussions of historic, existing, and proposed gun legislation.

GunCite
http://www.guncite.com
This gun-rights website contains many links to essays, articles, statistics, and opinions about gun control.

Gun Owners of America
https://gunowners.org/
Gun Owners of America is a nonprofit lobbying organization formed to preserve and defend the Second Amendment rights of gun owners. Visitors will find news and opinion pieces written about the latest in gun-control legislation.

March for Our Lives
https://marchforourlives.com/
March for Our Lives is a central base for youth-based gun-control advocacy and voter registration efforts. Find out about the latest planned protests, learn how to petition politicians, where and how to register to vote, and how to connect with allies in your area.

National Rifle Association Institute for Legislative Action
http://www.nraila.org
The NRA-ILA is the lobbying arm of the National Rifle Association. Its mission is to preserve the gun rights of all Americans. Its website includes information on proposed gun laws and provides overviews of state and federal gun laws.

PAX: The Center to Prevent Youth Violence
http://paxusa.org
PAX is an organization working to end the crisis of youth violence in the United States. PAX develops public health and safety campaigns that promote the simple steps parents, kids, teachers, and others can take to prevent youth violence. The website provides resources on preventing gun violence, as well as a wealth of gun violence statistics.

Second Amendment Foundation (SAF)
http://www.saf.org
The Second Amendment Foundation is a gun-rights organization dedicated to promoting understanding of the Second Amendment. The website offers detailed breakdowns of legal cases involving gun law, as well as resources to help visitors protest proposed gun control.

Violence Policy Center
http://www.vpc.org
The Violence Policy Center works to reduce gun violence through research, political advocacy, and education. Its website includes resources about the gun lobby, as well as news on legislation and the latest incidents of gun violence.

INDEX

American Revolution, 15–16, 37
ammunition, 19, 34, 71, 81
    armor-piercing bullets, 23, 69, 75–76
    and Gun Control Act of 1968, 22
    regulation of, 59, 63, 82
    state-level restrictions, 76
    types of, 75–76
arming teachers, 92–93
    infographic, 89
assassinations and guns
    John F. Kennedy, 22
    Robert Kennedy, 22
    Martin Luther King Jr., 22
    Lee Harvey Oswald, 22
    Ronald Reagan, 24
assault weapons, 25–26, 69–73
    types of, 69–71
automatic weapons, 19, 68
    AK-47, 70
    AR-15, 66–67, 70
    and bump stocks, 69–70
    and civilians, 76
    and federal assault weapons ban, 26, 71–73, 76
    and Second Amendment, 70
    and semiautomatic weapons, 25–26, 71

background checks, 30–31, 61, 64, 69, 82, 85–87
    and Brady Handgun Violence Prevention Act (1993), 24–25, 82
    and National Instant Criminal Background Check System, 82–84
    and straw purchases, 78–79, 83
ballistic imaging, 81
bans, 10, 13, 20, 23–24, 58, 60, 69–70, 76
    and federal assault weapons ban, 26, 71–73
Bill of Rights, 6, 8–9, 17–18, 94
    See also Second Amendment
Brady Campaign to Prevent Gun Violence, 24
bump stocks, 69–70

castle laws, 49
court cases, 61–63, 95
    District of Columbia v. Heller, 25–26, 57–59
    United States v. Lopez, 89
    United States v. Miller, 68–69
crime prevention
    and guns, 19–22, 24–26, 38–39, 88
    and self-defense, 37, 46–48, 88
    statistics, 44–45, 63–64, 84, 90
defensive gun uses, 26, 31, 37, 46–49, 57–59, 75–77
    and gun control, 17–18, 76

and minimum necessary force, 49–51
statistics, 47

Everytown for Gun Safety, 5, 43, 55, 64

Federal Bureau of Investigation, 9, 33,
    38, 42, 50, 52–54, 64
    and background checks, 25, 82–84

Giffords Law Center to Prevent Gun
    Violence, 44, 63–64
    and Gabrielle Giffords shooting,
    44–45
gun buybacks, 90–91
gun control, 7–9, 13, 19–27, 36–39, 53,
    64–65, 82–86, 91–93
    infographic, 33, 64
    and Thomas Jefferson, 17–18
    and mental illness, 8, 32, 54, 61–63
    and the Second Lateran Council, 10
    and Donald Trump, 30–32, 62–63,
    90, 92–93
gun culture
    in colonial America, 13–16
    and gun shows, 86
    in the New Nation, 16–17, 57
gun dealers, 20, 22–25, 65, 81–83, 85
gun deaths
    and access to guns, 8–9
    accidental, 39–43, 63–64
    infographics, 9, 38–39, 42, 64
    murders, 18, 43–44
    statistics, 7, 37, 48
    US global ranking, 37–39
    among youth, 37, 63–65
    See also suicides
gun-free zones, 88–90
    and mass shootings, 90
    and schools, 89–90
gun laws, 4, 18–19, 21, 27, 30, 43–44,
    61–64, 79–82, 91–92
    Brady Handgun Violence Prevention
    Act (1993), 24–25, 82, 88
    concealed carry, 80, 86–88
    in Europe, 14, 36–37
    federal, 55–56, 59–60, 63, 70–71,
    79–82, 95
    Federal Assault Weapons Ban (1994),
    71–73

Federal Firearms Act (1938), 20
Firearm Owners' Protection Act
    (1986), 23–24, 81–82
Gun Control Act (1968), 21–22, 53,
    76, 81–82
Gun-Free Schools Act (1994), 89
Gun-Free School Zones Act (1990), 89
Gun Show Background Check Act
    (2009), 86
Gun Show Loophole Closing Act
    (2009), 86
Gun Show Loophole Closing Act
    (2017), 86, 88
Law Enforcement Officers Protection
    Act (1985), 23
Mailing of Firearms Act (1927), 19
in Mexico, 38–39
National Firearms Act (1934), 19–20,
    68–69
in the New Nation, 16–18
Protection of Lawful Commerce in
    Arms Act (2005), 65
state, 6, 15, 31–32, 49–50, 80–82,
    84
Undetectable Firearms Act (1988), 24
and the US Supreme Court, 26,
    57–59, 68–69, 89, 95
Violent Crime Control and Law
    Enforcement Act (1994), 26
gunlock programs, 43
gunlocks, 43
    and the NRA, 43
    Project Child Safe, 43
gun ownership
    and criminals, 7–8, 19, 23, 25, 37–39,
    56–57, 59–60, 76, 83–84, 88–90
    and dementia, 62
    and felons, 20, 24, 52, 59–60, 78,
    83, 88
    and Gun Control Act of 1968, 21–22,
    53, 76, 81–82
    and mental illness, 8, 32, 54, 61–63
    and the No Fly List, 52–53, 56
    reasons for, 14, 16, 36, 46, 57, 69
    and self-defense, 9, 26, 46–49, 59,
    75
    and straw purchases, 78–79, 83
    and terrorists, 52–56, 70

and youth, 63–65
gunpowder
   history of, 11–12
gun rights, 6–9, 20–21, 52–53, 93–94
   collective, 8, 26, 37, 56–59
   in colonial America, 14–16
   in Europe, 13–14, 17, 36–37
   history of, 10–33
   individual, 8, 26, 33, 56–59
   infographic, 33
guns, 8–9
   and the American Revolution, 15–16
   history of, 11–13, 67–68
   and law enforcement, 23, 48, 57, 76, 78–81, 91–93
   and organized crime, 19–20
   and self-defense, 9, 26, 46–49, 59, 75
   and teachers, 92–93
   types of, 69–75
   and warfare, 8, 15–17, 77
gun safety, 9, 63–65, 79–80
   education, 42, 65
gun shows, 85–86
   and federal firearms lincensees, 85
   and gun culture, 86
   and gun show loophole, 82, 86, 88
   and legislation, 24
gun technology, 8, 12–13, 81
   high-tech models, 7, 43
   and mechanization, 18–19
   and Second Amendment, 67–68
gun violence
   and Dee and Darrell Hill shooting, 62
   and domestic abuse, 43–44, 54, 59–60, 88
   and duels, 18
   and Gabrielle Giffords shooting, 44–45
   and hate crimes, 31, 66–67
   and indigenous peoples, 13–15, 57
   infographics, 9, 38–39, 42, 64
   and Trayvon Martin shooting, 31

handguns, 12–13, 19–22, 24, 26–27, 58, 63–64, 68, 73, 78, 87–88
   and self-defense, 31, 75, 77
hate crimes
   Trayvon Martin shooting, 31

Tree of Life synagogue shooting, 66–67
heavy artillery, 76–77
   regulation of, 77
   types of, 76–77

infographics
   duty-to-retreat laws, 50
   gun control vs. gun rights, attitudes toward, 33
   gun deaths, in relation to gun laws, 64
   gun deaths, types of, 42
   guns in schools, attitudes toward, 89
   US gun deaths by state, 9
   US gun deaths vs. other nations, 38–39

liability
   and gun dealers, 65
   and gun manufacturers, 43, 65
   and the Protection of Lawful Commerce in Arms Act (2005), 65
licensing and registration, 19–20, 79–82
   and Federal Firearms License, 82, 85–86
   and gun dealers, 24–25, 82

March for Our Lives, 4–6
   protest marches, 4–6, 30, 95
   youth activism, 4–7, 30, 94–95
mass shootings, 5–6, 26–30, 32, 63, 70, 87–88, 90, 92
   First Baptist Church (Sutherland Springs, TX), 34–36
   Pulse Nightclub (Orlando, FL), 28–29
   Route 91 Harvest music festival (Las Vegas, NV), 28, 67
   Tree of Life synagogue shooting (Pittsburgh, PA), 66–67
microstamping
   California law, 81
   and Smith & Wesson, 81

National Rifle Association (NRA), 6, 19–26, 30–32, 34–36, 43, 55–56, 90, 92
   American Rifleman, 21–22
   financial clout, 21, 62, 73, 87
   history of, 21–24

political influence, 4, 6, 21, 23–24,
30, 62, 73, 94–95
and Second Amendment rights,
54–56, 68–71, 80, 92
and Donald Trump, 30–32, 90

red flag laws, 91–92
and Marjory Stoneman Douglas school
shooting, 92
regulatory agencies
Bureau of Alcohol, Tobacco, Firearms
and Explosives, 22

school shootings, 4–5, 94
Columbine High School (Columbine,
CO), 5
Marjory Stoneman Douglas High
School (Parkland, FL), 4–7, 28–30,
61–62, 92–93, 95
Perry Hall High School (Perry Hall,
MD), 93
Sandy Hook Elementary School
(Newton, CT), 26–28
Second Amendment, 7–8, 18, 36, 44,
54–55, 67–70, 80, 84–85, 90, 92
and Bill of Rights, 6, 17
interpretation of, 8, 56–57, 59–60,
76–77
and militias, 8, 57
and NRA, 20–22, 30–32, 55, 86–87
US Supreme Court cases, 26, 57–59,
68–69, 95
wording of, 8–9
self-defense and guns, 9, 14, 26,
46–49, 59, 75–76
castle laws, 49
duty to retreat, 48–50
minimum necessary force, 49–51
stand-your-ground laws, 31
semiautomatic weapons, 25, 73–74
AK-47, 70
AR-15, 66–67, 70
and mass shootings, 34, 36, 66–67
regulation of, 25–26, 69, 71, 81
types of, 69, 71
stand-your-ground laws, 48–50
and Trayvon Martin shooting, 31
straw purchases, 78–79, 83

suicides, 44–46, 91–92
and guns, 7, 42, 44–46, 75
Kerry Lewiecki, 46
and waiting periods, 45–46, 84

terrorists
and gun control, 52–56, 70
3D printable guns, 81
and security detection, 24
Trump, Donald, 30, 62–63
and arming teachers, 92–93
and the NRA, 30–32, 90, 95

views on gun-free zones, 89–90
views on guns, 6, 9, 12, 60

waiting periods, 69, 84–85
and homicide reduction, 24–25, 84
and Second Amendment rights,
84–85

ABOUT THE AUTHOR

Matt Doeden has written hundreds of children's and YA books on topics ranging from American history and sports to conflict resolution and current events. His YA title *Darkness Everywhere: The Assassination of Mohandas Gandhi* was a Children's Book Committee at Bank Street College Best Children's Book of the Year. Two of his recent YA sports titles, *The World Cup: Soccer's Global Championship* and *The Super Bowl: Chasing Football Immortality,* were Junior Library Guild picks and garnered star reviews from *Kirkus Reviews.* Doeden lives in Minnesota with his wife and two children.

PHOTO ACKNOWLEDGMENTS

Image credits: Design: d13/Shutterstock.com (background); AlanVec /Shutterstock.com. Content: NICHOLAS KAMM/AFP/Getty Images, p. 5; Drew Angerer/Getty Images, p. 7; Laure Westlund/Independent Picture Service, pp. 9, 33, 38–39, 40–41, 42, 50, 64, 89; Florilegius /Alamy Stock Photo, p. 11; Dirck Halstead/The LIFE Images/Getty Images, p. 25; Kevin Moloney/Getty Images, p. 27; Chip Somodevilla /Getty Images, p. 28; Daniel Munoz/Getty Images, p. 28; Ben Gabbe /Paramount Network/Getty Images, p. 31; Nicholas Kama/AFP/Getty Images, p. 33; Scott Olson/Getty Images, p. 35; Alex Wong/Getty Images, p. 45; EDUARDO MUNOZ ALVAREZ/AFP/Getty Images, p. 47; Andy Cross/ The Denver Post/Getty Images, p. 53; Tom Williams/Roll Call/Getty Images, p. 58; Dia Dipasupil/Vanity Fair/Getty Images, p. 63; BRENDAN SMIALOWSKI/AFP/Getty Images, p. 67; George Frey/Getty Images, p. 70; David Becker/Getty Images, p. 72; Kelly West/AFP /Getty Images, p. 74; Win McNamee/Getty Images, p. 79; Spencer Platt/ agency/Getty Images, p. 85; David McNew/agency/Getty Images, p. 91; Irfan Khan/Getty Images, p. 95.

Cover: Rob Crandall/Shutterstock.com; d13/Shutterstock.com (background); AlanVec/Shutterstock.com (target).